W9-BDB-549

Capitalism 3.0

Capitalism 3.0

A GUIDE TO RECLAIMING THE COMMONS

PETER BARNES

BERRETT-KOEHLER PUBLISHERS, INC.
San Francisco
a BK Currents book

Berrett-Koehler Publishers, Inc.
235 Montgomery Street, Suite 650
San Francisco, CA 94104-2916
Tel: (415) 288-0260   Fax: (415) 362-2512   www.bkconnection.com

Ordering Information
Quantity sales. Special discounts are available on quantity purchases by nonprofit organizations, corporations, associations, and others. For details, contact the "Special Sales Department" at the Berrett-Koehler address above.
Individual sales. Berrett-Koehler publications are available through most bookstores. They can also be ordered directly from Berrett-Koehler: Tel: (800) 929-2929; Fax: (802) 864-7626; www.bkconnection.com
Orders for college textbook/course adoption use. Please contact Berrett-Koehler: Tel: (800) 929-2929; Fax: (802) 864-7626.
Orders by U.S. trade bookstores and wholesalers. Please contact Publishers Group West, 1700 Fourth Street, Berkeley, CA 94710. Tel: (510) 528-1444; Fax (510) 528-3444.

Berrett-Koehler and the BK logo are registered trademarks of Berrett-Koehler Publishers, Inc.

Printed in the United States of America
Berrett-Koehler books are printed on long-lasting acid-free paper. When it is available, we choose paper that has been manufactured by environmentally responsible processes. These may include using trees grown in sustainable forests, incorporating recycled paper, minimizing chlorine in bleaching, or recycling the energy produced at the paper mill.

Library of Congress Cataloging-in-Publication Data
Barnes, Peter.
    Capitalism 3.0 : a guide to reclaiming the commons / by Peter Barnes.
       p. cm.
    Includes bibliographical references and index.
    ISBN-10: 1-57675-361-1; ISBN-13: 978-1-57675-361-3
       1. Commons—United States. 2. Privatization—United States. 3. Capitalization—United States. I. Title.
HD1289.U6B37 2006
333.2—dc22   2006013322

First Edition
11 10 09 08 07 06   10 9 8 7 6 5 4 3 2 1

Interior Design: Laura Lind Design   Proofreader: Henrietta Bensussen
Copy Editor: Sandra Beris   Indexer: Medea Minnich
Production: Linda Jupiter, Jupiter Production

To Cornelia and Smokey

For his labor being the unquestionable

property of the laborer,

no man but he can have a right

to what that is once joined to,

at least where there is enough, and as good,

left in common for others.

—*John Locke (1690)*

Contents

Preface

I'm a businessman. I believe society should reward successful initiative with profit. At the same time, I know that profit-seeking activities have unhealthy side effects. They cause pollution, waste, inequality, anxiety, and no small amount of confusion about the purpose of life.

I'm also a liberal, in the sense that I'm not averse to a role for government in society. Yet history has convinced me that representative government can't adequately protect the interests of ordinary citizens. Even less can it protect the interests of future generations, ecosystems, and nonhuman species. The reason is that most—though not all—of the time, government puts the interests of private corporations first. This is a *systemic* problem of a capitalist democracy, not just a matter of electing new leaders.

If you identify with the preceding sentiments, then you might be confused and demoralized, as I have been lately. If capitalism as we know it is deeply flawed, and government is no savior, where lies hope?

This strikes me as one of the great dilemmas of our time. For years the Right has been saying—nay, *shouting*—that government is flawed and that only privatization, deregulation, and tax cuts can save us. For just as long, the Left has been insisting that markets are flawed and that only government can save us. The trouble is that both sides are half-right and half-wrong. They're both right that markets and state are flawed, and both wrong that salvation lies in either sphere. But if that's the case, what are we to do? Is there, perhaps, a missing set of institutions that can help us?

I began pondering this dilemma about ten years ago after retiring from Working Assets, a business I cofounded in 1982. (Working Assets offers telephone and credit card services which automatically donate to nonprofit groups working for a better world.) My initial ruminations focused on climate change caused by human emissions of heat-trapping gases. Some analysts saw this as a "tragedy of the commons," a concept popularized forty years ago by biologist Garrett Hardin. According to Hardin, people will always overuse a commons because it's in their self-interest to do so. I saw the problem instead as a pair of tragedies: first a tragedy of the market, which has no way of curbing its own excesses, and second a tragedy of government, which fails to protect the atmosphere because polluting corporations are powerful and future generations don't vote.

This way of viewing the situation led to a hypothesis: if the commons is a *victim* of market and government failures, rather than the *cause* of its own destruction, the remedy might lie in strengthening the commons. But how might that be done? According to prevailing wisdom, commons are inherently difficult to manage because no one effectively owns them. If Waste Management Inc. owned the atmosphere, it would charge dumpers a fee, just as it does for terrestrial landfills. But since no one has title to the atmosphere, dumping proceeds without limit or cost.

There's a reason, of course, why no one has title to the atmosphere. For as long as anyone can remember there's been more than enough air to go around, and thus no point in owning any of it. But nowadays, things are different. Our spacious skies aren't empty anymore. We've filled them with invisible gases that are altering the climate patterns to which we and other species have adapted. In this new context, the atmosphere is a scarce resource, and having someone own it might not be a bad idea.

But who should own the sky? That question became a kind of Zen koan for me, a seemingly innocent query that, on reflection, opened many unexpected doors. I pondered the possibility of starting a planet-saving, for-profit, sky-owning business; after all, I'd done well by doing good before. When that didn't seem right, I wondered what would happen if we, as a society, created a trust to manage the atmosphere on behalf of future generations, with present-day citizens as secondary beneficiaries. Such a trust would do exactly what Waste Management Inc. would do if it owned the sky: charge dumpers for filling its dwindling storage space. Pollution would cost more and there'd be steadily less of it. All this would happen, after the initial deeding of rights to the trust, without government intervention. But if this trust—not Waste Management Inc. or some other corporation—owned the sky, there'd be a wonderful bonus: every American would get a yearly dividend check.

This thought experiment turned into a proposal known as the *sky trust* and has made some political headway. It also served as the epicenter of my thinking about the commons, which led to this book.

A Personal Exploration

The exploring that lies behind this book began long before I started Working Assets. As a boy, I helped my father crunch numbers for several books he wrote about the stock market. Later, as a journalist for *Newsweek* and *The New Republic,* I wrote dozens of articles on economic issues. But my real economic education began in my thirties, when, after a midlife crisis, I abandoned journalism and plunged headfirst into capitalism.

My motives at the time were mixed. On one level, I was tired of writing, needed money, and didn't like working for other people. On another level, I wanted to see if various ideas I'd acquired made sense. I'd been much affected by the writings of British economist E. F. Schumacher. In his 1973 book *Small Is Beautiful,* Schumacher argued that capitalism is dangerously out of sync with both nature and the human psyche. As an alternative, he envisioned an economy of small-scale enterprises, often employee-owned, using clean technologies.

With Schumacher's vision in mind, I leapt into action. Along with five friends, I started a solar energy company owned cooperatively by its employees. The company flourished until changes in tax law wiped out the nascent solar industry in the 1980s. By then, I was knee-deep into a twenty-year second career, during which I started mutual funds and telephone companies, served on boards of banks and manufacturers, and invested in numerous other businesses. The unifying theme of all these ventures was that they sought to earn a profit and improve the world at the same time. Their managers were strongly committed to multiple bottom lines: they knew they had to make a profit, but they also had social and environmental goals.

For much of this time I was president of Working Assets, a company that donates 1 percent of its gross sales to nonprofit groups working for a better world. These donations come off its top line, not its bottom line; the company makes them whether it's profitable or not (and many years we were not). It occurred to me that 1 percent is an exceedingly small portion of sales for any business to return to the larger world, given that businesses *take* so much from the larger world without paying. How, for example, could we make any goods without nature's many free gifts? And how could we *sell* them without society's vast infrastructure of laws, roads, money, and so on? At the very least, I liked to think, we ought to pay a 1 percent royalty for the privilege of being a limited liability corporation.

I also entertained a notion that, by showing other companies that they *could* give back 1 percent of their sales and survive, Working Assets could spark a movement that would improve the world. It was a pipe dream, I confess, but not entirely without logic. My thinking was that the 1 percent give-back was like a mutant gene added to our DNA. If it survived in the marketplace, it could spread. At employee orientations, I used to say that our company was seeking to make socially responsible genes the dominant business genes of the future.

Eventually, after retiring from Working Assets in 1995, I began reflecting on the profit-making world I'd emerged from. I'd tested the system for twenty years, pushing it toward multiple bottom lines as far as I possibly could. I'd dealt with executives and investors who truly cared about nature, employees, and communities. Yet in the end, I'd come to see that all these well-intentioned people, even as their numbers grew, couldn't shake the larger system loose from its dominant bottom line of profit.

In retrospect, I realized the question I'd been asking since early adulthood was: *Is capitalism a brilliant solution to the problem of scarcity, or is it itself modernity's central problem?* The question has many layers, but explorations of each layer led me to the same verdict. Although capitalism started as a brilliant solution, it has become the central problem of our day. It was right for its time, but times have changed.

When capitalism started, nature was abundant and capital was scarce; it thus made sense to reward capital above all else. Today we're awash in capital and literally running out of nature. We're also losing many social arrangements that bind us together as communities and enrich our lives in nonmonetary ways. This doesn't mean capitalism is doomed or useless, but it does mean we have to modify it. We have to adapt it to the twenty-first century rather than the eighteenth. And that can be done.

How do you revise a system as vast and complex as capitalism? And how do you do it *gracefully,* with a minimum of pain and disruption? The answer is, you do what Bill Gates does: you upgrade the operating system.

Scope of the Book

Much as our Constitution sets forth the rules for government, so our economic operating system lays down the rules for commerce. I use the possessive *our* to emphasize that this economic operating system belongs to everyone. It's not immutable, and we have a right to upgrade it, just as we have a right to amend our Constitution. This book tells why we must upgrade it, what a new operating system could look like, and how we might install it.

The book has three parts. Part 1 focuses on our current operating system, a version I call *Capitalism 2.0*. (Capitalism 1.0 died around 1950, as I'll explain in chapter 2.) I show how this system devours nature, widens inequality, and makes us unhappy in the process. Although many readers will already be aware of these problems, I examine them anew to show that these outcomes aren't accidental—they're inescapable consequences of our economic software. This means they can't be fixed by tinkering at the edges. If we want to fix them, we have to change the code.

Part 2 of the book focuses on capitalism as it could be, a version I call *Capitalism 3.0*. The key difference between versions 2.0 and 3.0 is the inclusion in the latter of a set of institutions I call the *commons sector*. Instead of having only one engine—that is, the corporate-dominated private sector—our improved economic system would run on two: one geared to maximizing private profit, the other to preserving and enhancing common wealth.

These twin engines—call them the corporate and commons sectors—would feed and constrain each other. One would cater to our "me" side, the other to our "we" side. When properly balanced—and achieving that balance would be government's big job—these twin engines would make us more prosperous, secure, and content than our present single engine does or can. And it would do this without destroying the planet.

Part 2 proposes a number of new property rights, birthrights, and institutions that would enlarge the commons sector in one way or another. I like to think that these proposals blend hope and realism. Among them are:

- A series of ecosystem trusts that protect air, water, forests and habitat;
- A mutual fund that pays dividends to all Americans—one person, one share;
- A trust fund that provides start-up capital to every child;
- A risk-sharing pool for health care that covers everyone;
- A national fund based on copyright fees that supports local arts;
- A limit on the amount of advertising.

The final part of the book explains how we can get to Capitalism 3.0 from here, how the models can work, and what you and I can do to help.

The *dramatis personae* throughout the book are corporations, government, and the commons. The plot goes something like this. As the curtain rises, corporations are gobbling up the commons. They're the big boys on the block, and the commons—an unorganized mélange of nature, community, and culture—is the constant loser. It has no property rights of its own, so must rely on government for protection. But government is a fickle guardian that tilts heavily toward corporations.

Fortunately, corporations only dominate government *most* of the time; every once in a while, they lose their grip. So it's possible to imagine that the next time corporate dominance ebbs, government—acting on behalf of commoners—swiftly fortifies the commons. It assigns new property rights to commons trusts, builds commons infrastructure, and spawns a new class of genuine co-owners. When corporations regain political dominance, as they inevitably will, they can't undo the new system. The commons now has safeguards and stakeholders; it's entrenched for the long haul. And in time, corporations accept the commons as their business partner. They find they can still make profits, plan farther ahead, and even become more globally competitive.

None of the proposals advanced in this book will come to fruition tomorrow. My aim, though, is not that. My aim is to light a beacon, to show the kind of system we should be building, bit by bit, as opportunities arise. I see this system-building as a decades-long process punctuated by periods of rapid change. It will involve businesses and politicians, economists and lawyers, citizens and opinion leaders at all levels. If we're not to get lost, we'll need a guide, and that's what I hope this book will be.

Acknowledgments

The ideas expressed in this book have been forming for a lifetime. I'm therefore indebted to many more people than I can name.

Of those I shall name, my late parents are first. My mother, Regina, was a feisty English teacher; my father, Leo, a thoughtful economist. It's no wonder I've pursued careers in journalism and business, and am now writing about economics. I owe my passion and grammar to one, my inquisitiveness and logic to the other.

My partner, Cornelia Durrant, made this book happen. Many of the keenest insights, when not Smokey's, were hers.

My editor, Johanna Vondeling, understood this book from the beginning, and kept it on track. Thanks also to Steve Piersanti and the entire BK staff, and to John de Graaf for introducing me to BK.

Seth Zuckerman wrestled clarity from an unruly draft. Without him I would not have met my deadline. I'm also extremely grateful to the Rockefeller Foundation, which provided a much-needed retreat for writing in Bellagio, Italy.

My fellow Fellows at the Tomales Bay Institute—Jonathan Rowe and David Bollier, in particular—were a constant source of ideas and encouragement. So, whether they knew it or not, were Dean Baker, Harriet Barlow, Connie Best, James Boyce, Rachel Breen, Marc Breslow, Peter Brown, Chuck Collins, Chris Desser, Peter Dorman, Brett Frischmann, Robert Glennon, Charles Halpern, Ann Hancock, Lewis Hyde, Marjorie Kelly, George Lakoff, Frances and Anna Lappé, Kathleen Maloney, Neil Mendenhall, David Morris, Richard Norgaard, Matt Pawa, Carolyn Raffensperger, Julie Ristau, Mark Sommer, Allen White, Bob Wilkinson, Susan Witt, and Oran Young.

Others whose writings have influenced me include E. F. Schumacher, Herman Daly, John Maynard Keynes, John Kenneth Galbraith, Ronald Coase, Louis Kelso, and Henry George.

This entire undertaking would not have been possible without the love and support of my entire family, especially Eli and Zack. Thank you so much.

Part 1

THE PROBLEM

Chapter 1

Time to Upgrade

Society is indeed a contract . . . between those who are living,
those who are dead, and those who are to be born.
— Edmund Burke (1792)

For the first time in history, the natural world we leave our children will be frightfully worse than the one we inherited from our parents. This isn't just because we're using the planet as if there were no tomorrow—that's been going on for centuries. It's because the cumulative weight of our past and present malfeasance has brought us to several tipping points. Nature has her tolerance limits, and we've reached many of them. In some cases, very possibly, we've passed them.

The State of the World

Consider, for example, our atmosphere. It's not just today's pollution that hurts, it's the accumulation of fumes we've been pouring into the air for centuries. This has already caused ice caps to melt, hurricanes to gain ferocity, and the Gulf Stream to weaken. Almost universally, the world's scientists warn that far worse lies ahead. The question our generation faces is: will we change our economic system voluntarily, or let the atmosphere change it for us?

Consider also what scientists call *biodiversity.* The earth is a tiny island of life in a cold, dark universe. We humans share this magical island with millions of other species, most of whom we haven't met. Each of these species fills a niche and contributes to the web of life. Yet little by little, we're pushing the others out of their living spaces. The result is a wave of extinctions comparable to that which wiped out the dinosaurs sixty-five million years ago. The difference is that, while the dinosaurs' extinction was triggered by a freak event, the current extinctions are being caused by our everyday activities.

And it's not just other species we're endangering. As anthropologists Jared Diamond and Ronald Wright recently reminded us, past human civilizations (Sumer, Rome, the Maya, Easter Island) did on a smaller scale what our own economic system seems bent on doing planet-wide: they destroyed their resource bases and crashed. The pattern is hauntingly familiar. First, the civilization finds a formula—agriculture, irrigation, fishing, capitalism—for extracting value from ecosystems. Because the formula works so well, the civilization's leaders become blindly attached to it. Eventually, the key resources on which the formula depends become depleted and the inflexible civilization collapses like a house of cards.

I'm not suggesting we're doomed to repeat this pattern. Because we can revise our economic operating system, we have a chance to avert it. But let's not belittle the risks we face today—they're real and imminent. And the time we have left to upgrade our operating system is limited.

What I Mean By the Commons

When most people think of the commons, they imagine a pasture where animals graze. That's an antiquated notion, and not what I have in mind. In this book I use *the commons* as a generic term, like *the market* or *the state.* It refers to all the gifts we inherit or create together.

This notion of the commons designates a set of assets that have two characteristics: they're all gifts, and they're all shared. A gift is something we receive, as opposed to something we earn. A shared gift is one we receive as members of a community, as opposed to individually. Examples of such gifts include air, water, ecosystems, languages, music, holidays, money, law, mathematics, parks, the Internet, and much more.

These diverse gifts are like a river with three tributaries: *nature, community,* and *culture* (see figure 1.1). This broad river precedes and surrounds capitalism, and adds immense value to it (and to us). Indeed, we literally can't live without it, and we certainly can't live well.

There's another quality to assets in the commons: we have a joint obligation to preserve them. That's because future generations will need them to live, and live well, just as we do. And our generation has no right to say, "These gifts end here." This shared responsibility introduces a moral factor that doesn't apply to other economic

Figure 1.1
THE THREE FORKS OF THE COMMONS RIVER

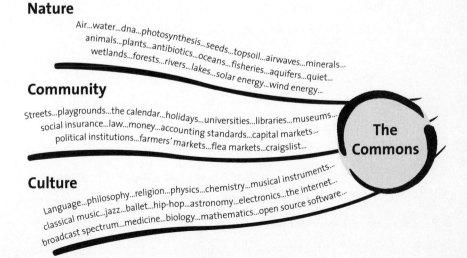

Nature
Air...water...dna...photosynthesis...seeds...topsoil...airwaves...minerals... animals...plants...antibiotics...oceans...fisheries...aquifers...quiet... wetlands...forests...rivers...lakes...solar energy...wind energy...

Community
Streets...playgrounds...the calendar...holidays...universities...libraries...museums... social insurance...law...money...accounting standards...capital markets... political institutions...farmers' markets...flea markets...craigslist...

The Commons

Culture
Language...philosophy...religion...physics...chemistry...musical instruments... classical music...jazz...ballet...hip-hop...astronomy...electronics...the internet... broadcast spectrum...medicine...biology...mathematics...open source software...

assets: it requires us to manage these gifts with future generations in mind. Markets don't naturally do this. If an asset yields a competitive return to capital, markets keep it alive; otherwise, they let it die. No other factors matter.

Assets in the commons are meant to be preserved *regardless of their return to capital.* Just as we receive them as shared gifts, so we have a duty to pass them on in at least the same condition as we received them. If we can add to their value, so much the better, but at a minimum we must not degrade them, and we certainly have no right to destroy them.

Besides the commons, I use a few similar-sounding terms that should be clarified here as well.

- By *common wealth* I mean the monetary and nonmonetary value of all the assets in the commons. Like stockholders' equity in a corporation, it may increase or decrease from year to year depending on how well the commons is managed.
- By *common property* I mean a class of human-made rights that lies somewhere between private property and state property. Like private property, common property arises when the state recognizes it. Unlike private property, it's *inclusive* rather than *exclusive*—it strives to share ownership as widely, rather than as narrowly, as possible.
- By *the commons sector* I mean an organized sector of our economy. It embraces some of the gifts we inherit together, but not all. In effect, it's a subset of the given commons that we consciously organize according to commons principles. It's small at the moment, but the point of this book is that we should enlarge it.

The Tragedy of the Commons Isn't What You Think

If you heard about the commons before you picked up this book, your impressions were probably shaped by a 1968 article called "The Tragedy of the Commons." In that article, biologist Garrett Hardin used the metaphor of an unmanaged pasture to suggest a root cause of many planetary problems.

> *The rational herdsman concludes that the only sensible course for him to pursue is to add another animal to his herd. And another. . . . But this is the conclusion reached by each and every rational herdsman sharing a commons. Therein is the tragedy. Each man is locked into a system that compels him to increase his herd without limit—in a world that is limited. Ruin is the destination toward which all men rush, each pursuing his own best interest. . . . Freedom in a commons brings ruin to all.*

Hardin's notion of tragedy was taken from philosopher Alfred North Whitehead, who in turn drew upon Aristotle. According to Whitehead, the essence of tragedy is "the remorseless working of things." In Hardin's view, commons are fated to self-destruct. There's nothing humans can do in the context of the commons to halt this inexorable outcome.

Hardin was right about humanity's unrelenting destruction of nature, but wrong about its cause and inexorability. He blamed the commons itself, when the true destroyer was, and remains, forces outside the commons. In Hardin's hypothetical, the commons does nothing to protect itself against those forces. It's completely unmanaged. But there's no inherent reason why commons *can't* be managed as commons.

Contrary to the picture painted by Hardin, medieval European commons (which included not only pastures but forests and streams) were far from unmanaged. They had rules barring access to outsiders and limiting use by villagers. For example, a rule that persists today in many Swiss villages is that villagers can't graze in common pasture more animals than they can feed over winter on their own land. A *managed* commons, in other words, isn't inherently self-destructive. The real danger to the commons is enclosure and trespass by outsiders.

Our Economic Operating System

An operating system is a set of instructions that orchestrates the moving parts of a larger system. The most familiar example is a computer operating system that coordinates the keyboard, screen, processor, and so on. Operating system instructions are written in code that can reside in electrons (as in a computer), chemicals (as in genes), or social norms and laws. Frequently, parts of the code can be expressed mathematically.

Just as our Constitution sets the rules for our democracy, so our economic operating system sets the rules for capitalism. Our economic operating system isn't as widely understood as our Constitution, nor is it spelled out in one concise document. It's visible if you look for it, but it's hidden in a shroud of statutes and court decisions. Still, like the Constitution, it's *there*—and it runs the mercantile life of our nation.

I like to think of our economic operating system as analogous to the rules of the board game *Monopoly*. It defines such things as starting conditions, rules of play, and the distribution of rewards and risk. It defines them partly through law, and partly by assigning fictional things called *property* and *money*.

All operating systems contain feedback loops—if certain conditions are detected, do this; if others are detected, do that. These feedback loops can be virtuous (the reaction fixes the problem) or vicious (the reaction makes the problem worse). A stable system has lots of virtuous loops and is good at weeding out vicious loops.

Sometimes, in human-made systems, virtuous loops have to be consciously added. Consider the steam engine of eighteenth-century inventor James Watt. Watt's design included two critical mechanisms: the steam-driven engine itself, and a centrifugal governor to keep the engine from getting out of control. When the latter detects a potentially dangerous behavior—speeding—it automatically corrects that behavior.

Illth and Thneeds

More than a century ago, English economist John Ruskin observed that the same economic system that creates glittering wealth also spawns what he called *illth*—poverty, pollution, despair, illness. It makes life comfortable for some, but does so at considerable discomfort to others.

Modern economists' term for illth is *negative externalities.* By this they mean the costs of economic transactions that are "external" to the parties involved. The classic example is a factory that dumps effluent into a river. Unlike homeowners who pay for garbage pickup, the factory's owners pay nothing for disposing their waste into the river. But humans and other creatures living downstream do pay a cost. Plants and animals suffer and die, while cities have to build expensive treatment plants. From the standpoint of the factory owner, none of this matters. But from the standpoints of nature and society, these are negative externalities. (There can, sometimes, be positive externalities—for example, if your neighbor repaints her house, that may increase the value of yours.)

For a long time, economists assured us that the wealth spewed out by our economic machine was so great, and the illth so trivial, that we didn't need to worry about negative externalities. If this was ever true, it's assuredly true no longer. Contemporary climate change is, quintessentially, a problem of negative externalities. We pay owners of land beneath which fossil fuels lie. We pay drillers, refiners, transporters, and retailers. But we don't pay nature, or anyone else, for dumping heat-trapping gases into the atmosphere. We shift this cost to our children, and take a free ride. We party, they pay.

What's more, many negative externalities aren't even the result of meeting genuine human needs. The word *thneed* doesn't appear in any economics text, but it's symbolic of our modern predicament. The word was coined by Theodor Geisel—better known as Dr. Seuss—in his children's fable *The Lorax*. A *thneed* is a thing we want but don't really need. As many parents will recall, *The Lorax* pits a dynamic entrepreneur (the Once-ler) against a pesky Lorax who "speaks for the trees." The Once-ler makes thneeds by cutting down truffula trees. When the Lorax protests, the Once-ler replies:

> *I'm being quite useful. This thing is a Thneed.*
> *A Thneed's a Fine-Something-That-All-People-Need!*

Economists have no technical term for *thneed*; they assume that all "demand" in the economy is equivalent, as long as it's backed with money. Yet surely it would be helpful to differentiate. One can imagine an axis running from needs to thneeds. On one end are such things as food, shelter, basic transportation, and health care. On the other end are Coca-Cola, iPods, and Hummers. (Significantly, needs are generic, while thneeds are typically branded.) Filling needs contributes more to human well-being than does selling thneeds, yet our economic system increasingly devotes scarce resources to thneeds.

Why do we have so much illth and so many thneeds? Because our economic operating system is far out of balance. On one side, representing owners of capital, are powerful profit-maximizing corporations. On the other side, representing future generations, nonhuman species, and millions of humans with unmet needs, are— almost nothing. The system lacks institutions that preserve shared inheritances, charge corporations for degrading nature, or boost the "demanding" power of people whose basic needs are ignored. Hence the system generates ever more illth, waste, and ever-widening disparities between rich and poor.

Upgrading Our System

Can we imagine, design, and install an upgraded operating system that fixes these flaws? This may seem a far-fetched dream. But consider that something comparable happened before, in 1935, with the enactment of Social Security.

Like the changes I'm suggesting here, Social Security is an intergenerational compact, engraved into our economic operating system. It was imagined, designed, and installed early in the twentieth century in response to what was then a looming crisis: the impoverishment of millions too old to work. The basic contract was, and remains, simple: active workers collectively support retired workers, and in return are supported in old age by the next generation of workers. For seventy years, this contract has been administered without scandal or waste by a trust fund that has never missed a payment. Thanks to this operating system upgrade, extreme old-age poverty, once rampant, is largely a thing of the past.

What we need now is a comparable system upgrade, this time to fix capitalism's disregard for nature, future generations, and the nonelderly poor.

Premises of This Book

All thought processes start with premises and flow to conclusions. Here are the main premises of this book.

1. WE HAVE A CONTRACT

Each generation has a contract with the next to pass on the gifts it has jointly inherited. These gifts fall into three broad categories: nature, community, and culture. The first category includes air, water, and ecosystems. The second includes laws, infrastructure, and many systems by which we connect with one another. The third includes language, art, and science. All of these gifts are immensely valuable, and need to be preserved if not enhanced.

2. WE ARE NOT ALONE

We living humans could benefit from a bit more humility. Not only do our children and grandchildren matter, so do other beings and their offspring. They have a right to be here, even if they aren't useful to us. An economic system should represent their interests as well as ours. A practical way to do this is needed.

3. ILLTH HAPPENS

Poverty, pollution, despair, and ill-health—what John Ruskin called *illth*—is the dark side of capitalism. This dark side needs to be addressed.

4. FIX THE CODE, NOT THE SYMPTOMS

If we want to reduce illth on an economy-wide scale, we need to change the code that produces it. Ameliorating symptoms after the fact is a losing strategy. Unless the code itself is changed, our economic machine will always create more illth than it cleans up. Moreover, illth prevention is a lot cheaper than illth cleanup.

5. REVISE WISELY

Most of what's in our current code is fine as is, and shouldn't be tinkered with. "If it ain't broke, don't fix it," is a valid maxim. What *does* need fixing should be fixed gradually whenever possible, as fairly as possible, and at the lowest cost possible. Efficiency and grace matter.

6. MONEY ISN'T EVERYTHING

Money is the blood of our economic system; it shouldn't be the soul. Humans have needs and desires that can't be met by exchanging dollars. These needs include connection to family and community, closeness to nature, and meaning in life. A twenty-first-century economic system must address these needs, too. This doesn't mean it must fill them directly; often, the best it can do is leave space for them to be filled in nonmonetary ways. What it shouldn't do is *get in the way* of their being met.

7. GET THE INCENTIVES RIGHT

Notwithstanding the above, an economic system works best when it rewards desired behavior. As Mary Poppins put it, "A spoonful of sugar helps the medicine go down" (and as I've never forgotten, offering a free pint of Ben & Jerry's was the best way Working Assets ever found to get customers). While we're looking for methods to protect nature and future generations, we need to make the incentives work for living humans as well.

If you disagree with any of these premises, you're unlikely to fancy my conclusions. If, on the other hand, these premises make sense to you, then welcome to these pages. I won't bore you with statistics, or tell you, yet again, that our planet is going to hell; I'm tired, as I suspect you are, of numbers and gloom. Nor will I tell you we can save the planet by doing ten easy things; you know it's not that simple. What I *will* tell you is how we can retool our economic system, one step at a time, so that after a decent interval, it respects nature and the human psyche, and still provides abundantly for our material needs.

Perhaps capitalism will always involve a Faustian deal of some sort: if we want the goods, we must accept the bads. But if we must make a deal with the devil, I believe we can make a much better one than we presently have. We'll have to be shrewd, tough, and bold. But I'm confident that, if we understand *how* to get a better deal, we *will* get one. After all, our children and lots of other creatures are counting on us.

Chapter 2

A Short History of Capitalism

They hang the man and flog the woman
That steal the goose from off the common,
But let the greater villain loose
That steals the common from the goose.

—English folk poem, ca. 1750

Before we consider how to upgrade our economic operating system, it's worth contemplating how it came to be. Two parallel threads emerge: the decline of the commons and the ascent of private corporations.

The Decline of the Commons

In the beginning, the commons was everywhere. Humans and other animals roamed around it, hunting and gathering. Like other species, we had territories, but these were tribal, not individual.

About ten thousand years ago, human agriculture and permanent settlements arose, and with them came private property. Rulers granted ownership of land to heads of families (usually males). Often, military conquerors distributed land to their lieutenants. Titles could then be passed to heirs—typically, oldest sons got everything. In Europe, Roman law codified many of these practices.

Despite the growth in private property, much land in Europe remained part of the commons. In Roman times, bodies of water, shorelines, wildlife, and air were explicitly classified as *res communes,* resources available to all. During the Middle Ages, kings and feudal lords often claimed title to rivers, forests, and wild animals, only to have such claims periodically rebuked. The Magna Carta, which King John of England was forced to sign in 1215, established forests and fisheries as *res communes.* Given that forests were sources of game, firewood, building materials, medicinal herbs, and grazing for livestock, this was no small shift.

In the seventeenth century, John Locke sought to balance the commons and private property. Like others of his era, he saw that private property doesn't exist in a vacuum; it exists in relationship to a commons, vis-à-vis which there are takings and leavings. The rationale for private property is that it boosts economic production, but the commons has a rationale, too: it provides sustenance for all. Both sides must be respected.

Locke believed that God gave the earth to "mankind in common," but that private property is justified because it spurs humans to work. Whenever a person mixes his labor with nature, he "joins to it something that is his own, and thereby makes it his property." But here Locke added an important proviso: "For this labor being the unquestionable property of the laborer," he wrote, "no man but he can have a right to what that is once joined to, at least where there is enough, and as good, left in common for others." In other words, a person can acquire property, but there's a limit to how much he or she can rightfully appropriate. That limit is set by two considerations: first, it should be no more than he can join his labor to, and second, it has to leave "enough and as good" in common for others. This was consistent with English common law at the time, which held, for example, that a riparian landowner could withdraw water for his own use, but couldn't diminish the supply available to others.

Despite Locke's quest for balance, the English commons didn't last. In the eighteenth and nineteenth centuries, the movement to enclose and privatize it accelerated greatly. According to historian Karl Polanyi, this enclosure was the great transformation that launched the modern era. Local gentry, backed by Parliament, fenced off village lands and converted them to private holdings. Impoverished peasants then drifted to cities and became industrial workers. Landlords invested their agricultural profits in manufacturing, and modern times, economically speaking, began.

One observer of this transformation was Thomas Paine, America's pro-independence pamphleteer. Seeing how enclosure of the commons benefited a few and disinherited many others, Paine proposed a remedy—not a reversal of enclosure, which he considered necessary for economic reasons, but compensation for it.

Like Locke, Paine believed nature was a gift of God to all. "There are two kinds of property," he wrote. "Firstly, natural property, or that which comes to us from the Creator of the universe—such as the earth, air, water. Secondly, artificial or acquired property—the invention of men." In the latter, he went on, equality is impossible, but in the former, "all individuals have legitimate birthrights." Since such birthrights were diminished by enclosure, there ought to be an "indemnification for that loss."

Paine therefore proposed a "national fund" that would do two things:

> *[Pay] to every person, when arrived at the age of twenty-one years, the sum of fifteen pounds sterling, as a compensation in part, for the loss of his or her natural inheritance, by the introduction of the system of landed property: And also, the sum of ten pounds per annum, during life, to every person*

now living, of the age of fifty years, and to all others as they shall arrive at that age.

A century and a half later, America created a national fund to do part of what Paine recommended—we call it Social Security. We've yet to adopt the other part, but its basic principle—that enclosure of a commons requires compensation—is as sound in our time as it was in Paine's.

In the years since European settlement, America developed its own relationship with the commons, which in our case included the vast unfenced lands we took from native people and Mexico. Some Americans saw our commons as the soil from which to build a nation of educated small proprietors. They passed laws such as the Land Ordinance of 1785, the Homestead Act, the Morrill Land Grant College Act, and the Reclamation Act, which allocated family-size plots to settlers and financed schools to educate them. Many also cherished these lands for their wildness and beauty; they created national parks and wilderness areas.

At the same time, others in America lured Congress into endless giveaways, acquired huge chunks of the commons for themselves, and made fortunes. Two vignettes, occurring more than a century apart, illustrate this continuing process.

In 1877, Congress passed the Desert Land Act, which removed several hundred square miles from settlement under the Homestead Act. The lands were said to be worthless, and were to be sold for 25 cents an acre to anyone promising to irrigate them. In fact, much of the land was far from worthless. A chunk of it eyed by James Haggin and Lloyd Tevis—two cronies of California Senator Aaron Sargent—was located near the Kern River, and was partially settled already. By hiring vagabonds to enter phony claims, and then transferring those claims to themselves, Haggin and Tevis acquired 150 square miles before anybody else in California had even heard of the Desert Land Act. Oil was later found beneath the land, conferring a huge windfall on the heirs of the two land-grabbers.

In 1995, Congress decided it was time for Americans to shift from analog to digital television. This required a new set of broadcast frequencies, and Congress obligingly gave them—free of charge—to the same media companies to which it had previously given analog frequencies free of charge. Senator Bob Dole, the Republican leader, declared: "It makes no sense that Congress would create a giant corporate welfare program. . . . The bottom line is that the spectrum is just as much a national resource as our national forests. That means it belongs to every American equally." But, as they had before, the media companies got their free airwaves anyway.

If an accounting could be made, private appropriations of the commons in America alone would be worth trillions of dollars. The plot is almost always the same: when a commons acquires commercial value, someone tries to grab it. In the old days, that meant politically connected individuals; nowadays, it means politically powerful corporations. What's astonishing about these takings isn't that they occur, but how unaware of them the average citizen is. As former Secretary of the Interior Walter Hickel said, "If you steal $10 from a man's wallet, you're likely to get into a fight, but if you steal billions from the commons, co-owned by him and his descendants, he may not even notice."

Enclosure, in which property rights are literally taken or given away, is half the reason for the commons' decline; the other half is a form of trespass called *externalizing*—that is, shifting costs *to* the commons. Externalizing is as relentless as enclosure, yet much less noticed, since it requires no active aid from politicians. It occurs quietly and

Enclosure + Externalizing

continuously as corporations add illth to the commons without permission or payment.

The one-two punch of enclosure and externalizing is especially potent. With one hand, corporations take valuable stuff *from* the commons and privatize it. With the other hand, they dump bad stuff *into* the commons and pay nothing. The result is profits for corporations but a steady loss of value for the commons.

The Ascent of Corporations

When I speak in this book of corporations, I'm speaking of a very special institution: the publicly traded stock corporation. This is an institution with a board of directors, a set of executive officers, and a fluctuating set of shareholders to whom the directors and officers are legally accountable. These corporations have an explicit mission: to maximize return to stock owners.

When Adam Smith wrote *The Wealth of Nations* in 1776, there were barely a handful of corporations in Britain or America. The dominant business form was the partnership, in which small groups of people known to each other ran businesses they co-owned. In the public's mind—as in Smith's—the corporate form, in which managers sold stock to strangers, was inherently prone to fraud. Numerous scandals supported this view. Yet as the scale of enterprise grew, partnerships proved unable to aggregate enough capital. The great advantage of corporations was that they *could* raise capital from strangers. In this, they were aided by laws limiting stockholders' liability to the amounts they had invested.

In early America, state legislatures retained some control over corporations by granting charters to them one at a time. Typically, the charter specified a business—such as building a canal and then charging tolls—that a corporation was authorized to conduct. The corporation could do nothing else, and after a certain number of years, its charter expired.

These limitations didn't last long. By the mid-nineteenth century, corporations could live forever, engage in any legal activity, and merge with or acquire other corporations. In 1886, the U.S. Supreme Court declared that corporations were "persons" entitled under the Fourteenth Amendment to the same protections as living citizens. In effect, a corporate franchise became a perpetual grant of sovereignty, with the sovereign powers consisting of immortality, self-government, and limited liability.

These changes not only gave corporations great economic power; they conferred political power as well. Unlike average citizens, corporations have large flows of money at their disposal. With this money they can hire lobbyists, sway public opinion, and donate copiously to politicians. They can also sue, or threaten to sue, whenever it serves their needs. The one thing they can't do is vote, but with all their extra powers, voting is hardly necessary.

By the end of the twentieth century, corporate power—both economic and political—stretched worldwide. International agreements, promoted by the United States, not only lowered tariffs but extended corporate property rights and reduced the ability of sovereign nations to regulate corporations differently. In short, what corporations have wanted and largely won is a homogeneous global playing field around which they can freely move raw materials, labor, capital, finished products, tax-paying obligations, and profits.

All of this might be well and good, were it not for two things. First, despite the Supreme Court's holding, the modern corporation isn't a real person. Instead, it's an automaton designed to maximize profit for stockholders. It externalizes as many costs as it possibly can, not because it wants to, but because it *has* to. It never sleeps or slows down. And it never reaches a level of profitability at which it decides, "This is enough. Let's stop here."

The second difficulty is that these automatons keep getting bigger and more powerful. In 1955, sales of the Fortune 500 accounted for one-third of U.S. gross domestic product; by 2004 they commanded two-thirds. These few hundred corporations, in other words, enveloped not only the commons but also millions of smaller firms organized as partnerships or proprietorships (see figure 2.1).

Figure 2.1
WALL STREET VERSUS MAIN STREET, 1953–2000

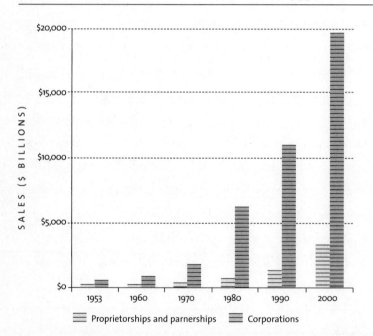

Source: *Historical Statistics of the United States, Colonial Times to 1970* (Washington, D.C.: U.S. Department of Commerce, Bureau of the Census, 1979). http://www2.census.gov/prod2/stat-comp/documents/; see 1970p2.zip. *Statistical Abstract of the United States* (Washington, D.C.: U.S. Department of Commerce, Bureau of the Census, 2005). http://www.census.gov/prod /2005pubs; see 06statab/business.

From Shortage to Surplus Capitalism

Sometime around 1950, capitalism entered a new phase. Until then, poverty was a widely shared American experience. Wages were low, hours were long, and unemployment was a wolf at almost every door. In the 1930s, it reached 25 percent.

This changed in the period following World War II. In 1958, economist John Kenneth Galbraith wrote a best-seller called *The Affluent Society* in which he noted that scarcity of goods was now a thing of the past for a majority of Americans. "The ordinary individual has access to amenities—foods, entertainment, personal transportation and plumbing—in which not even the rich rejoiced a century ago," Galbraith observed. "So great has been the change that many of the desires of the individual are no longer even evident to him. They become so only as they are synthesized, elaborated, and nurtured by advertising and salesmanship, and these, in turn, have become among our most important and talented professions."

This was a major phase change for capitalism. Before, people wanted more goods than the economy could provide. Demand, in other words, exceeded supply, and we lived in what might be called *shortage* capitalism. We could also call it Capitalism 1.0.

After the change, we shifted into *surplus* capitalism, or what I call Capitalism 2.0. In this version, there's no limit to what corporations can produce; their problem is finding buyers. A sizeable chunk of GDP is spent to make people want this unneeded output. And credit is lavishly extended so they can buy it.

This historic shift can be described another way. A century ago, our chief scarcity was goods. It thus made sense to sacrifice other things in pursuit of goods, and capitalism was masterful at doing this. Today we're waist-deep in thneeds, and our scarcities are different. Among the middle classes, the top scarcities, I'd say, are time, companionship, and community (see figure 2.2). Among the poor, there remains a lack of goods, but that lack isn't due to a shortage of production capacity—it's due to the poor's inability to pay. The critical scarcity here, in other words, is income.

Similarly, in the early capitalist era, land, resources, and places to dump wastes were abundant; aggregated capital was the scarcest factor. That's why rules and practices developed that put capital above all else. In the twenty-first century, however, this is no longer the case. As economist Joshua Farley has noted, "If we want more fish on our dinner plates, the scarce factor isn't fishing boats, it's fish. If we want more timber, the scarce factor isn't sawmills, it's trees."

As a businessman and investor, I've benefited personally from the primacy of capital and am not keen to end it. But as a citizen, I

Figure 2.2
LIFE UNDER SHORTAGE AND SURPLUS CAPITALISM

	1.0 SHORTAGE CAPITALISM	2.0 SURPLUS CAPITALISM
Scale	Local	Global
Supply and demand	Demand exceeds supply	Supply exceeds demand
Externalities	Low	High
Advertising	Minimal	Ubiquitous
Credit	Scarce	Abundant
Marginal value of more stuff	High	Low
Scarcities	Aggregated capital	Waste sinks, time, habitat, income, companionship, community

have to recognize that times have changed. The world is awash with capital, most of it devoted to speculation. By contrast, healthy ecosystems are increasingly scarce. If anything deserves priority, it's nature's capital, yet capitalism rolls on with financial capital as its king.

I should note that my numbering of capitalism's stages isn't meant to be definitive. I've heard some people say that capitalism has had three stages, and others that it's had four. Such counts are inevitably arbitrary. The point I wish to make is that capitalism changes. It's rigid in the sense that those who are privileged have plenty of power with which to protect their privileges, but it's not immutable. We've had at least two versions, and we can have another.

Three Pathologies of Capitalism

The anachronistic software that governs capitalism today leads, willy-nilly, to three pathologies: the destruction of nature, the widening of inequality, and the failure to promote happiness despite the pretense of doing so. Let's look at these pathologies separately, then explore how they're linked.

DESTRUCTION OF NATURE

Humans began ravaging nature long before capitalism was a gleam in Adam Smith's eye. Surplus capitalism, however, has exponentially enlarged the scale of that ravaging.

I promised no grim numbers, but I'll cite just one. In 2005, a United Nations–sponsored research team reported that roughly 60 percent of the ecosystems that support life on earth are being used unsustainably. Such overuse, reported the Millennium Ecosystem Assessment, increases the likelihood that abrupt, nonlinear changes will seriously affect human well-being. The potential consequences include floods, droughts, heat waves, fishery collapse, dead zones along coasts, sea level rises, and new diseases.

Thoughtful people can debate whether population or technology is more responsible than capitalism for our loss of ecosystems and biodiversity. No doubt all play a role. But most of the damage isn't done by the numerous poor; it's done by the far fewer rich. The United States, for example, with 5 percent of the world's people, has dumped nearly 30 percent of our species' cumulative carbon dioxide wastes into the atmosphere. It's our excess consumption, rather than the poor's meager gleanings, that's the larger problem, and surplus capitalism is the handmaiden of that excess.

Technology, of course, greatly magnifies our impact on the planet, but technology by itself is mere know-how. It's the *choice* of technologies, and the scale at which they're deployed, that affects the planet. Electricity, for example, can be generated in many ways. When corporations choose among them, however, their choice is driven not by "least harm to nature," but by "most bang for the buck." And, in doing their calculations, they count the cost of nature as zero. Hence we have lots of fossil-fuel burning and little use of solar, wind, and tidal energy.

The same calculus drives corporations' approach to agriculture, logging, and many other activities. The result is at once humbling and chilling: capitalism as we know it is devouring creation. It's living off nature's capital and calling it growth.

WIDENING OF THE GAP

Most Europeans who settled North America hoped to leave feudal inequities behind. They envisioned a competitive meritocracy rather than a permanent aristocracy. Unfortunately, it was not to be. Slavery was the first anomaly; it took a civil war to end that. Then came the epic grabs of land and robber barons, neither of which we've undone.

Fast-forward to my generation's watch. If ever there was a time when a rising tide should have lifted all boats, this was it. After World War II, America went on an almost uninterrupted growth binge. Per capita economic output, adjusted for inflation, tripled between 1950 and the end of the century. The stock market rose about fortyfold. Mutual funds and tax-sheltered retirement accounts spread stock ownership to the masses. In the 1960s, the federal government launched an all-out War on Poverty. And yet, at the end of the century, the distribution of private wealth was more unequal than it had been in 1950. In cold numbers, the top 5 percent owned more than the bottom 95 percent (see figure 2.3).

Figure 2.3
WEALTH DISTRIBUTION IN THE UNITED STATES, 2001

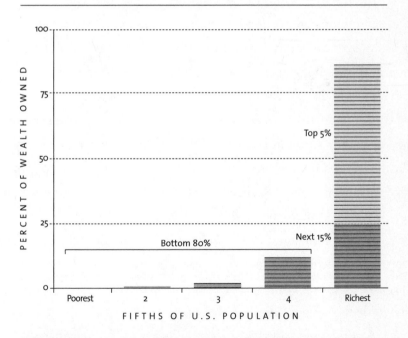

Source: Edward Wolff, Ajit Zacharias, and Asena Caner, *Levy Institute Measure of Economic Well-Being: United States, 1989, 1995, 2000, and 2001* (New York: Jerome Levy Economics Institute, May 2004). http://www.levy.org /default.asp?view=publications_view&pubID=fca3a44oee and http://students.washington.edu/ehirsh/documents/Inequality_figures.pdf.

Why did this happen? There are many explanations. One is that welfare kept the poor poor; this was argued by Charles Murray in his 1984 book *Losing Ground*. Welfare, he contended, encouraged single mothers to remain unmarried, increased the incidence of out-of-wed-lock births, and created a parasitic underclass. In other words, Murray (and others) blamed victims or particular policies for perpetuating poverty, but paid scant attention to why poverty exists in the first place.

There are, of course, many roots, but my own hypothesis is this: much of what we label private wealth is taken from, or co-produced with, the commons. However, these takings from the commons are far from equal. To put it bluntly, the rich are rich because (through corporations) they get the lion's share of common wealth; the poor are poor because they get very little.

Another way to say this is that, just as water flows downhill to the sea, so money flows uphill to property. Capitalism by its very design maximizes returns to existing wealth owners. It benefits, in particular, those who own stock when a successful company is young; they can receive hundreds, even thousands of times their initial investments when the company matures. Moreover, once such stockholders accumulate wealth, they can increase it through reinvestment, pass it on to their heirs, and use their inevitable influence over politicians to gain extra advantages—witness the steady lowering of taxes on capital gains, dividends, and inheritances. On top of this, in the last few decades, has been the phenomenon called *globalization*. The whole point of globalization is to increase the return to capital by enabling its owners to find the lowest costs on the planet. Hence the stagnation at the bottom alongside the surging wealth at the top.

A critical piece of this analysis is that very few *new* shares of corporate stock are issued. As author Marjorie Kelly has pointed out, most established corporations finance growth through retained earnings and debt. They're just as likely to buy back outstanding shares as to issue new ones. Consequently, old wealth is rarely diluted. When new money flows into the stock market, its main effect is to increase the wealth of existing stockholders and their fortunate heirs. Thus, of the total gain in marketable wealth that occurred in the United States between 1983 and 1998, more than half went to the top 1 percent.

The companies that do issue new stock are the young ones—the Microsofts, Apples, and Googles. Entertainers and athletes aside, most new multimillionaires are early stockholders in corporations like these. In these cases, however, the distribution of gains is so tilted in favor of these early stockholders that the skewed pattern of wealth distribution is replicated. New wealth joins old wealth, but the concentration remains the same. There's no mechanism for dispensing wealth—even new wealth—more evenhandedly.

WHY AREN'T AMERICANS HAPPY YET?

If thneeds were the path to happiness, most Americans would be delirious by now. But the accumulation of goods is only one means among many in the pursuit of human satisfaction. Everyone except economists seems to know this.

Economists take as a given that consuming more goods makes people happier, not just when they're poor, but at all times. Yet this assumption is not only illogical, it's contradicted by numerous surveys. Logically, the law of diminishing returns should apply here as elsewhere; as people acquire more goods, the marginal benefit of each additional good should decline toward zero. And research confirms this is so.

Since the early 1970s, the General Social Survey has asked Americans the same question: *Taken all together, how would you say things are these days—would you say you are very happy, pretty happy, or not too happy?* Though we've gotten considerably more accessorized since the

question was first asked, our answers have barely changed. In 1972,
31 percent of Americans considered themselves very happy; in 2004, it
was 33 percent (see figure 2.4). A noneconomist might conclude that,
if happiness is our goal, we've wasted trillions of dollars.

Why isn't economic growth making us happier? There are
many possibilities, and they're additive rather than exclusive. One is
that, once material needs are met, happiness is based on comparative
rather than absolute conditions. If your neighbors have bigger houses
than you do, the fact that yours is smaller diminishes your happiness,
even though your house by itself meets your needs. In the same way,
more income wouldn't make you happier if other people got even
more. That's why an affluent country can get richer without its
citizens getting happier.

A second reason is that surplus capitalism foments anxiety.
Millions live one paycheck, or one illness, away from disaster. When
disaster strikes, the safety nets beneath them are thin. And everyone
sees jobs vanishing as capital scours the planet for cheap labor.

Another reason is that surplus capitalism speeds up life and
creates great stress. Humans didn't evolve to multitask, sit in traffic
jams, or work, shop, and pay bills 24/7. We need rest, relaxation, and
time for companionship and creativity. Surplus capitalism can't give
us enough of those things.

Similarly, its nonstop marketing message—you're no good
without Brand X—breeds the opposites of gratitude and content-
ment, two widely acknowledged precursors of happiness. According
to the Union of Concerned Scientists, the average American encoun-
ters about three thousand such messages each day. No wonder we
experience envy, greed, and dissatisfaction.

Figure 2.4
HAPPINESS IN AMERICA, 1972–2004

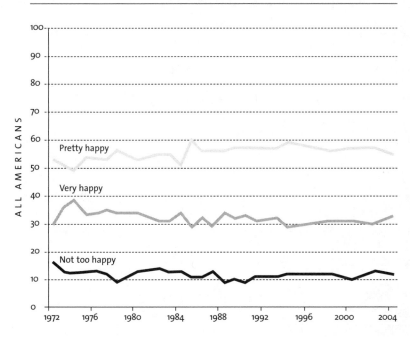

Source: http://pewresearch.org/social/chart.php?ChartID=37. Reprinted with permission of the Pew Research Center.

Waiting for 3.0

Let's summarize the history of capitalism thus far. Since arising in the eighteenth century, capitalism has changed the face and chemistry of the earth. It keeps doing so, despite signals of planetary peril, like a runaway steam engine without a governor. It has built mountains of private wealth, but much of that wealth was taken from the commons, and a great deal of it adds little to our happiness. Its main actors, profit-maximizing corporations, are essentially out of control, and the fruits of their exertions are dispensed in a highly unequal way.

Why does surplus capitalism behave this way? It's possible that we consistently hire bad CEOs, but I think otherwise. I think it's the *operating system* that causes most CEOs to act not with the next generation, but with the next quarterly statement, foremost in mind. This suggests that, if we want to change the outcomes of Capitalism 2.0, we have to upgrade its operating system.

In Part 2 I'll describe what a new operating system could look like. But first, in the next two chapters, I'll explain why other remedies, such as more regulation or more privatization, won't fix our current system's flaws.

Chapter 3

The Limits of Government

*Civil government, so far as it is instituted for the security of property,
is in reality instituted for the defense . . . of those who have
some property against those who have none at all.*
—Adam Smith, 1776

In his essay "The Tragedy of the Commons," Garrett Hardin envisioned only two ways to save the commons: *statism* and *privatism.* Either a coercive government would have to stop humans from mindlessly destroying the planet, or private property owners, operating in a free market, would have to do the job. In the next two chapters I'll show why neither of these approaches suffices.

In considering the potential of governmental remedies, let's clarify what we mean. We're not talking about tyranny; we're talking about legitimate forms of government activity such as regulation, taxation, and public ownership. Can these traditional methods effectively preserve common wealth for our children?

America's Two Experiments

The notion that government *should* protect the commons goes back a long way. Sometimes this duty is considered so basic it's taken for granted. At other times, it's given a name: the public trust. Several states actually put this duty in writing. Pennsylvania's constitution, for example, declares: "Pennsylvania's public natural resources are the common property of all the people, including generations yet to come. As trustee of these resources, the Commonwealth shall conserve and maintain them for the benefit of all the people." Note that in this constitutional dictum, serving as trustee of natural resources isn't an *option* for the state, it's an affirmative duty.

Yet here as elsewhere, rhetoric and reality differ. Political institutions don't function in a vacuum; they function in a world in which power is linked to property. This was true when fifty-five white male property owners wrote our Constitution, and it's no less true today.

America has been engaged in two experiments simultaneously: one is called democracy, the other, capitalism. It would be nice if these experiments ran separately, but they don't. They go on in the same bottle, and each affects the other. After two hundred years, we can draw some conclusions about how they interact. One is that capitalism distorts democracy more than the other way around.

The reason capitalism distorts democracy is simple. Democracy is an open system, and economic power can easily infect it. By contrast, capitalism is a gated system; its bastions aren't easily accessed by the masses. Capital's primacy thus isn't an accident, nor the fault of George W. Bush. It's what happens when capitalism inhabits democracy.

This isn't to say the United States government can't, at times, restrain corporations. It has a number of tools at its disposal, and has used them in the past with some success. But the measures it can take are woefully inadequate to the task of safeguarding the planet for our children. Let's see why.

Limits of Regulation

The idea of regulation is that, while markets should ideally be as free as possible, there are times when an external actor, not driven by profit maximization, must impose some rules for the common good.

When it comes to nature, government has many ways to regulate. It may require timely disclosure of toxic releases. It may grant, sell, or deny rights to use public resources. It may ban some pollutants altogether, limit others, or tell polluters what technologies to use. It may divide the landscape into zones and specify what kinds of activities can take place in each zone. It may tax certain activities and subsidize others.

This wide array of tools—plus the power to prosecute rule-breakers—seemingly creates in government a formidable counterweight to corporations. Yet history has shown that government isn't the regulatory tiger it appears to be. It faces fierce corporate resistance whenever it tries to exercise its powers. And time after time, its regulatory agencies have been captured by the industries they were intended to regulate.

The process of regulatory capture has been described by many scholars. Details vary, but the plot is always the same. A new agency is created to regulate an industry that's harming the public. At first the agency acts boldly, but over time its zeal wanes. Reformers who originally staffed the agency are replaced by people who either worked in the industry earlier, or hope to do so after a stint in government. Industry-packed "advisory committees" multiply, while industry-funded "think tanks" add a veneer of legitimacy to profit-driven proposals. Lobbyists meet constantly with agency staffers. The public, meanwhile, has no clue about what's going on.

This process has reached extreme proportions in recent years. As I write, the head of public lands in the Interior Department is a former mining industry lobbyist, the head of the air division at the EPA is a former utility lobbyist, the second in command at EPA is an ex-Monsanto lobbyist, and the head of Superfund cleanups at EPA (which makes industry clean up its toxic wastes) formerly advised companies on how to evade Superfund. Although today's pro-industry bias may be more egregious than usual, the absence of outrage or resistance suggests it's not far from the norm.

And it's not just regulatory agencies that have been captured. Congress itself, which oversees the agencies and writes their controlling laws, has been badly infected. According to the Center for Public Integrity, the "influence industry" in Washington now spends $6 billion a year and employs more than thirty-five thousand lobbyists, some two hundred of whom are former Congress members who enjoy easy access to their erstwhile colleagues.

A glimpse at the corporate lobbying game shows just how rewarding it is. MBNA, the nation's largest credit card bank, spent over $17 million on lobbying between 1999 and 2004. This is pin money compared to the sums it will reap from an industry-drafted bankruptcy overhaul, passed in 2005, which precludes all but the very poor from wiping out their debts and starting anew. (The great majority of Americans who file for bankruptcy are middle-class victims of job loss, huge medical bills, or family breakup.) A *New York Times* reporter described this scene as the bill was being marked up: "Lawyers and lobbyists jammed Congressional hearing rooms to overflowing. . . . During breaks, there was a common, almost comical pattern. The pinstriped lobbyists ran into the hallway, grabbed tiny cell phones from their pockets or briefcases, and reported back to their clients, almost always with the news they wanted to hear."

Or consider the biggest influence group in Washington these days, the pharmaceutical industry, which boasts more than two lobbyists for every member of Congress. "You can hardly swing a cat by the tail without hitting a pharmaceutical lobbyist," says Senator Chuck Grassley, chairman of the Senate Finance Committee. And with good reason: billions of dollars in drug company profits ride on actions taken—or not taken—by Congress. In 2003, for example, the industry won coverage for prescription drugs under Medicare, while blocking the government from negotiating prices downward. It kept Americans from importing cheaper medicines from Canada, and protected a system that uses company fees to speed the drug approval process.

Numbers can be put on this sort of thing, and Kevin Phillips, a former Republican strategist, has done so. "The timber industry spent $8 million in campaign contributions to preserve a logging road subsidy worth $458 million—the return on their investment was 5,725 percent. Glaxo Wellcome invested $1.2 million in campaign contributions to get a 19-month patent extension on Zantac worth $1 billion—their net return: 83,333 percent. The tobacco industry spent $30 million for a tax break worth $50 billion—the return on their investment: 167,000 percent. For a paltry $5 million in campaign contributions, the broadcasting industry was able to secure free digital TV licenses, a giveaway of public property worth $70 billion—that's an incredible 1,400,000 percent return on their investment."

The reason our political system works this way isn't that our politicians are particularly venal. Rather, the cause is structural. Industries that benefit from government favors are wealthy and well-organized. They earn high and immediate returns from lobbying expenditures and campaign donations. And just because the money isn't spent on outright bribes doesn't mean there aren't quid pro quos. Politicians and corporations have a symbiotic relationship. Politicians need money and corporations want favors. Neither side is dumb or shy. Politicians who hope for long careers won't often offend money suppliers. At a minimum they'll give them access, and in politics access is nine-tenths of the battle.

By contrast, ordinary citizens are cash-poor, unorganized, and ill-informed. They amble to the polls a few times per decade, if that. Of all the players in politics, they're the easiest to fool. And though politicians do read opinion polls, these rarely concern the arcane favors corporations seek. Hence, disciplined cash-rich corporations easily prevail over ordinary citizens.

There's even an economic theory explaining this: Mancur Olson's *logic of collective action.* Olson, a Harvard economist, argued that unless the number of players in a group is very small, people won't combine to pursue their common interests. For example, if the CEOs of five major airlines decide they want a $500 million government bailout, they pool their resources and hire a lobbying firm. Together they tell Congress that without the $500 million, their companies won't survive, and the consequences of their collapse will be dire.

Who lobbies against them? No one. The reason is that, while the five airlines will gain about $100 million each, the average taxpayer will lose only $5 each. It's thus not worth it for ordinary citizens to get off their duffs and fight.

On top of this, there's an even deeper problem. Democracy responds at best to voters and at worst to money. Both voters and donors are living humans. Not even seated at democracy's table—not organized, not propertied, and not enfranchised—are future generations, ecosystems, and nonhuman species. James Madison and his brethren could scarcely have foreseen this defect. In their day, politics was about the clash between living factions, not between living humans and their heirs, or between our species and the rest of nature. But that's no longer the case.

The implications of Adam Smith's quote at the beginning of this chapter are thus even graver than he thought. If government's inherent bias is toward property owners, the losers aren't only the poor. The losers are also future generations, ecosystems, and non-human species, none of whom own any property at all. The only positive news here is that the converse might also be true: if future generations, ecosystems, and nonhuman species *did* own property, they might have some economic and political power.

Limits of Taxation

Let's set aside for a moment the question of whether government is inherently biased toward property and focus instead on a purely mechanical question: is taxation a good tool for preserving gifts of nature? I pose this question because economists have advocated "green taxes" for over eighty years, and it's time to move beyond this hoary panacea.

The idea of using taxes to protect nature dates back to 1920, when Cambridge University's top economist, Arthur Pigou, proposed it. At first blush the idea makes sense. If pollution is free, there'll be lots of it. If it's taxed, there'll be less. Taxation forces polluters to internalize some of the costs they'd otherwise externalize.

So far, so good. The devil, however, is in the details. For example, who sets the taxes? What algorithm do they use? How quickly can they act? To whom are they accountable? And where does the money go?

When the federal government sets taxes, the key players are the House Ways and Means Committee and the Senate Finance Committee. As any observer of Congress will tell you, the process of writing tax laws is ugly, contentious, and time-consuming. Bills are introduced, hearings held, politics unleashed. More than anything else, this is what keeps Washington's lobbyists on their cell phones.

What algorithm drives committee members when they write tax laws? Most often, it's what's best for their reelection. They're not economists, they're politicians. They want to please donors and voters. Protecting nature, or future generations, isn't foremost in their minds. Hence, pollution taxes will never be as high as they need to be.

Consider a real example here—carbon taxes. A tax on carbon emissions could, in theory, reduce global warming. But in order to make a difference, the tax would have to get extremely high. This means Congress would have to raise the prices of gasoline, natural gas, and electricity year after year, hitting every business and consumer in the pocketbook. That's an improbable scenario.

In most situations, mainstream economists would shout, "Politicians shouldn't set prices, markets should!" Prices should announce to the world, on any given day, what buyers are willing to pay and sellers are willing to accept. To the extent that government distorts or delays this process, it leads to inefficient allocation of scarce resources, not the least of which is Congress's own time.

So why did Pigou and his followers give the price-setting job to politicians? Because, in their minds, there was no alternative. *Someone* had to set prices for pollution, and they thought no one else could do it. But there *are* other options.

Consider, for example, the Federal Reserve Board, created in 1913 to manage the nation's money supply. The Fed is a hybrid entity. Technically, it's a corporation whose stock is owned by member banks. However, the seven members of its board of governors are appointed by the president and confirmed by the Senate to staggered fourteen-year terms. The genius of the Fed is that its governors can make tough economic decisions without risking defeat at the polls. In particular, they can raise interest rates, which means higher borrowing costs for businesses and higher mortgage and credit card payments for millions of voters. No politician wants to do this, and thanks to the Fed, none have to. When constituents complain about high interest rates, Congress members point to the Fed and say, "Talk to them." This model is so sensible that, nowadays, almost all countries use it.

One can imagine similar entities for managing carbon and other pollutants. Their governors would serve long terms and have a fiduciary responsibility to future generations. They could make tough economic decisions—such as raising energy prices—without committing political suicide. Such entities might appeal to elected politicians precisely because they permit a shifting of responsibility and blame.

And that's not the only alternative to political price-setting. We know from "cap-and-trade" programs that markets can set prices for pollution. In such systems, politicians have an important task—they set up the system and assign the initial property rights—but once they do that, they can be off the hook on prices.

Two other questions about pollution taxes are who pays them and where the money goes. There's little dispute about the first question. Consumers—which is to say, nearly everyone—pay them, even if the tax falls initially on polluters. That's because any pollution tax paid by a business will be passed on to consumers in the form of higher prices. Consumers can reduce what they pay by buying fewer products that cause pollution; to that extent, they can "evade" the tax, and such evasions will benefit nature. But many consumers have little choice about reducing or shifting their purchases; they *must* drive to work and heat their homes. And because low-income households spend virtually all of their incomes on unavoidable consumption, pollution taxes fall disproportionately on them.

As for the second question—where does the money go?—it goes to government coffers. Like any tax, a pollution tax takes money out of private pockets and turns it over to the state. It's then up to politicians to decide what to do with it. It's possible that politicians will use the money fairly and wisely, but there are no guarantees. If recent history is any guide, they'll use much of it to expand the military-industrial complex and lower taxes on campaign donors.

There's another, more fundamental reason why taxes are a poor tool for guarding nature. It's not higher pollution prices we want; what we actually want is less pollution. Taxes are at best a roundabout way to get there. We assume that if we raise pollution prices, pollution will come down. But not even the smartest economist can know how quickly it will come down, or by how much. We can only proceed by trial and error. Much of the tax-setters' time will be spent debating how much of a price hike will produce how much of a reduction in pollution, when in fact what we *should* be debating is how quickly we want pollution to drop. Once that debate is settled, we should be able to set a valve at the agreed-upon level. We can't do that with pollution taxes.

Pollution taxes, in short, though better than nothing, are far from an ideal way to protect nature. They'd make polluters internalize some of the costs they now shift to others, but in a clumsy, regressive, and ultimately insufficient way. If another way to internalize costs is possible, we should consider it.

Limits of Public Ownership

Because of historical circumstances, America has a long tradition of public land ownership. When Europeans first arrived, North America was held in common by an assortment of tribes. As these tribes were dispossessed, the federal government acquired their territories. Some of the federal holdings were given to states as they entered the union. Though most of what the federal and state governments owned was then sold cheaply, much was retained. Today, nearly a third of the land in the United States is government-owned.

To say that land—or any asset—is "government-owned," however, isn't to say it's managed on behalf of future generations, nonhuman species, or ordinary citizens. Consider what the federal and state governments have done with the lands they own.

Outside of Alaska, about 5 percent of government-owned lands have been designated as wilderness. In such areas, humans may enter on foot but not use motorized vehicles. Mining, logging, and hunting are also prohibited. On the other 95 percent of government-owned land, private and commercial use is regulated by various agencies. National forests are managed by the U.S. Forest Service, grazing and mineral lands by the Bureau of Land Management, hunting and fishing by the U.S. Fish and Wildlife Service.

As a general rule, politics—not fiduciary duty—determines what uses are permitted and what prices are charged. A classic example is the Mining Act of 1872, under which private companies can stake claims to mineral-bearing lands for $5 an acre, and pay no royalties on the minerals they extract. Every attempt to reform this antiquated law has failed because of the mining companies' political clout.

In the same vein, the U.S. Forest Service has for decades been selling trees to timber companies for below-market prices. On top of that, it spends billions of tax dollars building roads in virgin forests so timber firms can harvest the people's trees. This is, of course, economically irrational and a huge subsidy to private corporations. It also addicts Americans to cheap forest products and destructive logging methods. These practices occur because the Forest Service is not a trust committed to ecosystem preservation, but a politically influenced agency dedicated to "multiple use" of government-owned forests.

There are exceptions to this dismal pattern. One involves trust lands given by the federal government to states. Such gifts began with the Land Ordinance of 1785, which reserved one square mile per township for the support of public schools. Later, the Morrill Land Grant College Act of 1862 gave more land to states to support colleges of agriculture and mechanics. And in 1954, Congress gave Texas title to oil-rich coastal lands, providing that all revenue from them be placed in an endowment, or permanent fund, that generates income for public schools forever.

Today, twenty-two states hold about 155 million acres in trust for public schools and colleges—which is to say, for future genera-tions. Like the federal government, the state trusts lease much of their land for oil drilling, timber cutting, and cattle grazing. The trusts' duty is to preserve not the land itself but the income streams it gener-ates. This creates beneficiaries (educators, students, parents) who monitor the land managers closely. One result, according to Univer-sity of California professor Sally Fairfax, is that state trust lands are better managed than federally owned lands. Whereas the U.S. Forest Service "has been hiding the ball on cash flows and returns to invest-ments for most of this century . . . the state trust land managers know how to keep books and make them public." Further, even though the state trusts aren't bound to protect ecosystems per se, they tend to do so because they have a long-term calculus.

An interesting variant of the typical state land trust is the Alaska Permanent Fund, created in 1976 to absorb some of the windfall from leasing state land to oil companies. The aim was to create an endowment that would benefit Alaskans even after the oil is gone. To this end, the Permanent Fund invests in stocks, bonds, and similar assets, and off the earnings pays yearly dividends to every resi-dent. Originally, the dividends were to be allocated in proportion to the recipients' length of residence in Alaska, with old-timers getting more than newcomers. But the U.S. Supreme Court ruled that, because of the Equal Protection clause of the Fourteenth Amendment, Alaska couldn't discriminate against newcomers that way. The dividend formula was then changed to one person, one share.

Lessons for the Future

Three points are worth making here. First, ownership isn't the same thing as trusteeship. Owners of property—even government owners—have wide latitude to do whatever they want with it; a trustee does not. Trustees are bound by the terms of their trust and by centuries-old principles of trusteeship, foremost among which is "undivided loyalty" to beneficiaries.

Second, in a capitalist democracy, the state is a dispenser of many valuable prizes. Whoever amasses the most political power wins the most valuable prizes. The rewards include property rights, friendly regulators, subsidies, tax breaks, and free or cheap use of the commons. The notion that the state promotes "the common good" is sadly naive.

Third, while free marketers are fond of saying that capitalism is a precondition for democracy, what they neglect to add is that capitalism also distorts democracy. Like gravity, its tug is constant. The bigger the concentrations of capital, the stronger the tug.

We face a disheartening quandary here. Profit-maximizing corporations dominate our economy. Their programming makes them enclose and diminish common wealth. The only obvious counterweight is government, yet government is dominated by these same corporations.

One possible way out of this dilemma is to reprogram corporations—that is, to make them driven by something other than profit. This, however, is like asking elephants to dance—they're just not built to do it. Corporations are built to make money, and the truth

THE ALASKA PERMANENT FUND

Under Alaska's constitution, the state's natural resources belong to its people. Jay Hammond, Republican governor of Alaska in the 1970s, took this provision seriously. When oil began flowing from the North Slope, he pushed for royalties to be shared among Alaska's citizens. Many battles later, the legislature agreed to a deal: 75 percent of the state's oil revenue would go to the government as a replacement for taxes. The remaining 25 percent would flow into the Alaska Permanent Fund, and would be invested on behalf of all Alaskans equally.

Since 1982, the Fund has grown to over $30 billion and paid equal yearly dividends to all Alaskans, including children (see figure 3.1). In effect, it is a giant mutual fund managed on behalf of all Alaskan citizens, present and future. Even after the oil runs dry, it will continue to benefit everyone. Economist Vernon Smith, a Nobel laureate and libertarian scholar at the Cato Institute, has called it "a model [that] governments all over the world would be well-advised to copy."

Figure 3.1
ALASKA PERMANENT FUND DIVIDENDS

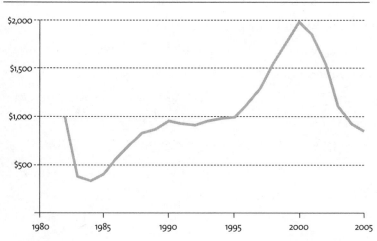

Source: Alaska Permanent Fund Corporation, http://www.apfc.org/alaska/dividendprgrm.cfm.

is, as a society we want them to make money. We'll look at this further in the next chapter.

Another possible way out is to liberate government from corporations, not just momentarily, but long-lastingly. This is easier said than done. Corporations have decimated their old adversary, organized labor, and turned the media into their mouthpiece. Occasionally a breakthrough is made in campaign financing—for example, corporations are now barred from giving so-called soft money to political parties—but corporate money soon finds other channels to flow through. The return on such investments is simply too high to stop them.

Does this mean there's no hope? I don't think so. The window of opportunity is small, but not nonexistent. Throughout American history, anticorporate forces have come to power once or twice per century. In the nineteenth century, we had the eras of Jackson and Lincoln; in the twentieth century, those of Theodore and Franklin Roosevelt. Twenty-first century equivalents will, I'm sure, arise. It may take a calamity of some sort—another war, a depression, or an ecological disaster—to trigger the next anticorporate ascendancy, but sooner or later it will come. Our job is to be ready when it comes.

What constitutes readiness? Three things, I believe. First, we must have a proper view of government's role. That role isn't to run the economy, or even to manage the commons directly; it's to assign common property rights to trustworthy guardians who will. Second, we must have a plan to fix our economic operating system, not just to put patches on symptoms. And third, we must recognize that the duration of any anticorporate ascendancy will be brief, and that we must use that small window to build institutions that outlast it.

Laws, regulations, and taxes are easily rescinded or weakened when corporations don't like them. Property rights, by contrast, tend to endure, as do institutions that own them. So we should focus on creating such institutions and endowing them with permanent property rights.

Make no mistake: it will take more than a few wand strokes to bring capitalism into harmony with nature and the human psyche. This is a thirty- to fifty-year project. During this time, we must be locked on a steady course. For this reason, I wouldn't place much faith in slim and fickle majorities in Congress. As we'll see, I *would* place it in the hands of commons trustees, empowered with property rights and bound as much as humanly possible to generations hence.

Chapter 4

The Limits of Privatization

The corporation is an externalizing machine, in the same way that a shark is a killing machine. There isn't any question of malevolence or of will. The enterprise has within it, as the shark has within it, those characteristics that enable it to do that for which it is designed.
—Robert Monks, 1998

It's tempting to believe that private owners, by pursuing their own self-interest, can preserve shared inheritances. No one likes being told what to do, and words like *statism* conjure fears of bureaucracy at best and tyranny at worst. By contrast, *privatism* connotes freedom.

In this chapter, we look at Garrett Hardin's second alternative for saving the commons: privatism, or privatization. I argue that private corporations, operating in unconstrained markets, can *allocate* resources efficiently but can't *preserve* them. The latter task requires setting aside some supplies for future generations—something neither markets nor corporations, when left to their own devices, will do. The reason lies in the algorithms and starting conditions of our current operating system.

The Algorithms of Capitalism 2.0

If you've ever used a computer spreadsheet, you know what an algorithm is. Each cell in the spreadsheet contains a set of instructions: take data from other cells, manipulate the data according to a formula, and display the result. The instructions within each cell are *algorithms.*

If you think of the economy as a huge spreadsheet, with each cell representing a producer, consumer, or property owner, you can see that the behavior of the whole is driven by the algorithms in the cells. Our current operating system is dominated by three algorithms and one starting condition. The algorithms are: (1) maximize return to capital, (2) distribute property income on a per-share basis, and (3) the price of nature equals zero. The starting condition is that the top 5 percent of the people own more property shares than the remaining 95 percent.

The first algorithm is what drives corporations. It tells them to sell as much as they can, pay as little as possible for labor, resources, and waste disposal, and make shareholders happy every quarter. It focuses the minds of managers every day. If they work in marketing, they wake up thinking about how to sell more; if there's no demand for their product, they must create some. If they work in finance, they worry about margins and leverage. If they're in labor relations, they bargain hard, replace long-term employees with temps, and shift jobs to places where wages are lower. All the while, the CEO feeds sweet numbers to Wall Street.

The second and third algorithms then mesh with the first. It's the combination of these algorithms that causes the wheels of capitalism to devour nature and widen inequality among humans. At the same time, nothing in the algorithms requires or encourages corporations, either individually or collectively, to preserve anything.

This doesn't mean people inside corporations don't think about protecting nature, raising their workers' pay, or giving something back to society. Often, they do. It *does* mean their room for actually doing such things is too narrow to make a difference. Nor does it mean that, from time to time, some brave mavericks don't briefly flout the corporate algorithm. They do that, too. What I'm saying is that, in the great majority of cases, the corporate algorithm and its brethren are obeyed. *For all practical purposes, the publicly traded corporation is a slave to its algorithm.*

Socially Responsible Corporations

To survive over time, every organization needs to take in more money than it spends. (The only possible exception may be the U.S. government.) This means that even nonprofit organizations must, in a sense, make a profit. But making a profit isn't the same as *maximizing* profit. In the first instance, profit is a means to an end; in the latter, it's the purpose that trumps all others. Millions of organizations earn enough money to stay alive, yet pursue goals other than profit. Is it possible for publicly traded corporations to be like that? Can they have *multiple* bottom lines? Can they, in other words, rise above their profit-maximizing algorithm?

There are several ways this might be possible: enlightened managers might choose a higher goal than profit, shareholders might insist on it, and government might require it. Let's consider each possibility.

ENLIGHTENED MANAGERS

Managers are human beings; they don't care just about money, they also care about the larger world. The problem is, they're trapped in a cold-hearted system. Managers are paid to do one thing, and to do it well. At best, they can be public-spirited as long as they don't harm the bottom line. This gives them *some* range to operate—for example, if using recycled paper adds minimally to their costs without reducing quality, they might use it. But if it adds substantially to their costs, they won't—or more accurately, *can't*—sacrifice profit for the sake of a few trees. What matters at the end of the day isn't the managers' personal values, but the difference in price between recycled paper and paper made from newly felled trees.

There are other reasons not to rely upon the voluntary benevolence of corporate executives. As *The Economist* has written, "The great virtue of the single bottom line is that it holds managers to account for something. The triple bottom line does not. It is not so much a license to operate as a license to obfuscate."

As a businessperson, I find this argument compelling. Every large organization, to be managed well, needs a mission. That mission should be as clear as possible. It's hard enough to manage to one bottom line; it's more than thrice as hard to manage to three. How do managers know, much less quantify, the external consequences of what they do? And even if they know, what do they do when goals conflict? Does profit trump nature or vice versa? If managers are accountable to shareholders for profit-based performance, to whom are they accountable for commons-based performance?

Hypothetical answers to such questions can no doubt be drafted, but what would happen in the real world, I suspect, is what *The Economist* surmises: profit maximization would dominate, accompanied by obfuscation about other goals. Corporate communications departments would try to maximize the *appearance* of social responsibility for the lowest actual cost. We'd see beautiful ads and reports, but little change in core behavior.

It's important to remember that the profit-maximizing algorithm is enforced not just by laws, but by a variety of carrots and sticks. For example, CEO compensation is typically based on a list of goals established by the board. These often include nonfinancial goals, but the goal that carries the most weight, and is least amenable to obfuscation, is profit. Further, the CEO and other top managers usually receive stock options. Since stock prices are driven by reported quarterly earnings, managers who own stock or stock options strive to maximize these.

When carrots fail to motivate, sticks come into play—and they can be brutal. An "underperforming" corporation will be devalued by the stock market. This makes it susceptible to takeover. A classic example is the Pacific Lumber Company of California, the largest private owner of old-growth redwood trees in the world. Prior to 1985, Pacific Lumber was a family-run business that took a long-term perspective. When it logged, it left up to half the trees standing, creating natural canopies and keeping much of the soil stable. It was also generous to its workers, renting them housing at below-market rates and refraining from layoffs during downturns.

Sadly, however, Pacific Lumber's responsible behavior made it easy prey for a takeover. Its concern for nature and its employees diminished its profits and hence its share price. Because of its cutting practices, it held tremendous stands of virgin redwoods that could be liquidated quickly. In addition, its pension plan was overfunded. Spotting all this, corporate raider Charles Hurwitz offered to buy the company in 1985 through a holding company called Maxxam. At first the directors refused, but when Hurwitz threatened to sue them for violating their fiduciary duty to shareholders, the directors succumbed.

Hurwitz financed his purchase with junk bonds, the interest on which was more than the historical profits of the company. To service this debt, he terminated the workers' pension plan and began harvesting trees at twice the previous rate. Such were the fruits of the previous managers' enlightened practices.

It *is* possible for a company to pursue multiple bottom lines if it's closely held by a group of like-minded shareholders—that was the case at my former company, Working Assets. But once a corporation goes public—that is, sells stock to strangers—the die is pretty much cast. Strangers want a stock that will rise when they plunk down their money, and profit is the sure path to doing that. It's just a matter of time, then, until the profit-maximizing algorithm kicks in.

I've spent a good part of my life talking with people who *wish* publicly traded companies could be socially responsible—not just cosmetically, but sufficiently to make a difference. They contend that corporations were once dedicated to public purposes, escaped their bounds, and can be put back in. They recall a time when companies were rooted in their communities, hired workers for life, and contributed to local charities. The trouble is, those days are irreversibly gone. Today, owners live nowhere near workers, labor and nature are costs to be minimized, and it's hard to see what might displace profit as the organizing principle for publicly traded corporations.

SOCIALLY RESPONSIBLE SHAREHOLDERS

Managers are ultimately responsible to shareholders, so if shareholders demanded social responsibility, perhaps managers would pay attention. That's the thinking behind socially responsible investing. Could *this* tactic tame corporations?

Partisans of this approach employ two techniques: screened investment (putting money in "good" companies and withholding it from "bad" ones) and shareholder activism. Screened investment funds have made considerable progress since I cofounded Working Assets Money Fund in 1983; they've grown from virtually nothing to over $2 trillion in assets, or approximately 10 percent of professionally managed money in the United States. These funds vet the corporations whose securities they buy, not just for financial performance but for social and ecological behavior as well. Their vetting process typically excludes firms that sell tobacco or alcohol, violate environmental regulations, discriminate against minorities, treat workers badly, or manufacture weapons. In theory, if enough people invested this way, they could lure corporations into behaving better than they otherwise might.

In reality, though, it hasn't worked like that, and doesn't seem likely to. One reason is that socially screened investment funds (with a few exceptions) aren't willing to accept a lower rate of financial return. "Doing well by doing good" is their mantra, and they strive to beat, or at least equal, the returns of funds that are not socially screened. When they succeed (and often they do), this "proves" that social responsibility makes good business sense. On the other hand, it means the funds can demand of companies only "good" behavior that enhances the bottom line. In this sense they're in the same narrow boat as managers who want to do good but can't if it hurts their profits.

A deeper reason for the funds' lack of impact may be found in this contradiction: as the funds get bigger, their screens necessarily get looser. If you have a few million dollars to invest, you can be picky about your nonfinancial criteria. If you have billions, you'll run out of places to put your money if you're too persnickety. Thus, as Paul Hawken has noted, over 90 percent of Fortune 500 companies now appear in portfolios that call themselves socially responsible, and the managers of those portfolios rarely bite the hands that feed them. Success, in this way, is its own undoing.

The second technique—shareholder activism—has also picked up steam in recent years. In this approach, concerned shareholders meet with top managers and urge them to change the company's ways. If the managers resist, the shareholders file resolutions that, if approved at an annual shareholder meeting, would change corporate policy. In 2003, over three hundred resolutions were submitted on issues ranging from CEO compensation to labor and environmental practices. None passed, because managers, through proxies, control the great majority of shares, although in some cases the resultant publicity did lead to changes.

A grander vision of shareholder activism involves the employee pension funds that, collectively, own over half the shares of many U.S. companies. In this vision, American workers, through their retirement funds, would require publicly traded corporations to place workers, communities, and nature on a par with short-term profit. In reality, pension funds *have* come to play a larger role in capital markets, but ironically, it's usually as the swing votes when raiders seek to take over underperforming corporations. In these situations, the pension funds often vote with raiders to enhance stockholder value.

Recently, pension funds have also pushed for improvements in corporate governance. But pension fund trustees are hardly *sans culottes* in pinstripes. They're tightly bound by their fiduciary responsibility to retirees, and must seek the highest rates of return or face reprisal from the U.S. Labor Department, which oversees them.

It would be a luscious irony if capital markets could become a check on runaway capitalism. But capital markets suffer from the same disease as corporations themselves—an incurable devotion to maximizing profit. This isn't to say that efforts to improve corporate responsibility are a waste of time; such efforts raise consciousness and are incrementally helpful. And they're certainly a form of right livelihood. But do they carry within them a systemic solution to the defects of capitalism? This I deeply doubt.

MANDATORY RESPONSIBILITY

I don't think it will ever happen, but consider this scenario. Imagine Congress passes a law requiring every corporation—in exchange for limited liability—to have a triple bottom line. The law also says that at least a third of corporate directors should represent workers, nature, and communities in which the company operates. And it protects directors from lawsuits if they favor nature over profit. You're the CEO of Acme Corporation. What changes do you make after the law takes effect?

Well, you might start by increasing your accounting budget. You'll need, henceforth, to keep track not only of money but also of your nonmonetary impacts on society and nature. This isn't easy, though presumably shortcuts will be developed. Next, you assign people to find ways to reduce Acme's negative impacts on nature and society, ranking the proposals by years to payback. You budget a modest sum for the most cost-effective projects, giving preference to those with public relations value. You publish ads and reports, patting yourself on the back for doing what the law requires. And you remind your board of directors that, if they choose, they can snub offers from the likes of Charles Hurwitz and forgo large capital gains for shareholders.

All this would be well and good. But given the algorithms that still rule, how much difference would it make? And even if it did have some effect, would it make enough difference in the right ways? After all, you might spend your small green budget on one thing, while nature most needs something else.

Now, as an alternative, imagine that the price of nature is no longer zero. All of a sudden, it costs big bucks to pollute or degrade ecosystems. Overnight, your managers scramble to cut pollution and waste. The higher the price, the faster their behavior changes. And it changes in response to specific natural scarcities, as indicated by specific prices.

The question is, which of these approaches would work better—mandatory social responsibility, or increases in the price of
nature? The answer, without doubt, is the latter.

Free Market Environmentalism

One other version of privatism is worth considering. Its premise is
that nature can be preserved, and pollution reduced, by expanding
private property rights. This line of thought is called *free market
environmentalism,* and it's favored by libertarian think tanks such as
the Cato Institute.

The origins of free market environmentalism go back to an
influential paper by University of Chicago economist Ronald Coase.
Writing in 1960, Coase challenged the then-prevailing orthodoxy
that government regulation is the only way to protect nature. In fact,
he argued, nature can be protected through property rights, provided
they're clearly defined and the cost of enforcing them is low.

In Coase's model, pollution is a two-sided problem involving
a polluter and a pollutee. If one side has clear property rights (for
instance, if the polluter has a right to emit, or the pollutee has a right
not to be emitted upon), and transaction costs are low, the two sides
will come to a deal that reduces pollution.

How will this happen? Let's say the pollutee has a right to clean
air. He could, under common law, sue the polluter for damages. To
avoid such potential losses, the polluter is willing to pay the pollutee a
sum of money up front. The pollutee is willing to accept compensation
for the inconvenience and discomfort caused by the pollution. They
agree on a level of pollution and a payment that's satisfactory to both.

It works the other way, too. If the polluter has the right to pollute, the pollutee offers him money to pollute less, and the same deal is
reached. This pollution level—which is greater than zero but less than

the polluter would emit if pollution were free—is, in the language of economists, *optimal.* (Whether it's best for nature is another matter.) It's arrived at because the polluter's externalities have been internalized.

For fans of privatism, Coase's theorem was an intellectual breakthrough. It gave theoretical credence to the idea that the marketplace, not government, is the place to tackle pollution. Instead of burdening business with page after page of regulations, all government has to do is assign property rights and let markets handle the rest.

There's much that's attractive in free market environmentalism. Anything that makes the lives of business managers simpler is, to my mind, a good thing—not just for business, but for nature and society as a whole. It's good because things that are simple for managers to do will get done, and often quickly, while things that are complicated may never get done. Right now, we need to get our economic activity in harmony with nature. We need to do that quickly, and at the lowest possible cost. If it's easiest for managers to act when they have prices, then let's give them prices, not regulations and exhortations.

At the same time, there are critical pieces missing in free market environmentalism. First and foremost, it lacks a solid rationale for how property rights to nature should be assigned. Coase argued that pollution levels will be the same no matter how those rights are apportioned. Although this may be true in the world of theory, it makes a big difference to people's pocketbooks whether pollutees pay polluters, or vice versa.

Most free marketers seem to think pollution rights should be given free to polluters. In their view, the citizen's right to be free of pollution is trumped by the polluter's right to pollute. Taking the opposite tack, Robert F. Kennedy Jr., an attorney for the Natural Resources Defense Council, argues that polluters have long been trespassing on common property and that this trespass is a form of subsidy that ought to end.

The question for me is, what's the best way to assign property rights when our goal is to protect a birthright shared by everyone? It turns out this is a complicated matter, but one we need to explore. There's no textbook way to "propertize" nature. (When I say to propertize, I mean to treat an aspect of nature as property, thus making it ownable. Privatization goes further and assigns that property to corporate owners.) In fact, there are different ways to propertize nature, with dramatically different consequences. And since we'll be living with these new property rights—and paying rent to their owners— for a long time, it behooves us to get them right.

Consider the matter of who represents pollutees. Coase presented his model in its simplest form: a single polluter and a single pollutee. In the real world, there are usually a few large polluters and millions of people who are polluted upon. It's prohibitively expensive for individual pollutees to sue large polluters, just as it is for large polluters to negotiate individually with pollutees.

For the Coasian model to work, the class of pollutees as a whole needs to be represented by an agent. What's more, it matters to whom that agent is accountable, and what principles drive its actions. If either the accountability or the principles are wrong, the agent will sooner or later do the wrong things. But if the agent's accountability and principles are *right*, we may actually have a fix for capitalism's predisposition to pollute. The key is to make each agent a trustee for future generations and all living citizens equally.

Then there's the matter of who gets the initial property rights, and whether or not they have to pay for them. Consider pollution trading as it's been put into practice so far. Government issues permits to dump a particular pollutant into the commons. It gives the permits—for free—to large polluters, based on how much they polluted in the past. Past polluters who reduce their future pollution can benefit by selling permits they no longer need.

This kind of pollution trading involves both propertization and privatization. First, a new kind of property is created—a right to emit a particular chemical into the commons. Then, this piece of property is given to private corporations. I have no problem with the first part of this process, propertization. What troubles me is the second part, privatization.

Giving away pollution permits, instead of auctioning them to the highest bidders, is like handing out free leases to an office building. Worse, it's like handing out free leases and letting the freeloaders sublease to others and pinch the rent. And we're not talking about pocket change, either. When it comes to carbon dioxide emissions, the assignment of property rights is potentially worth trillions of dollars. That's money consumers will inescapably pay in higher prices for energy. To *whom* they pay it depends on who gets the property rights to the sky.

Propertize, But Don't Privatize

Simply turning the commons over to corporations, without compensation or further ado, is like putting the fox in charge of the henhouse. There's no guarantee the corporations will preserve the asset, much less share its benefits widely. We're asked to *believe* that corporate owners will do the right things, either because it's in their self-interest or because they're socially responsible, but historical evidence and the inner logic of corporations suggest otherwise.

Nevertheless, it's possible to *propertize* a natural inheritance without privatizing it, and in the next chapter I'll show how this can work. The basic idea is to turn pieces of the commons into *common* property rather than corporate property. This would let us charge corporations higher (and truer) prices for using the commons, while sharing the benefits of those higher prices broadly. And it would ensure that the *quantity* of usage rights sold—which is to say, the level of pollution allowed—is set with the interests of future generations foremost in mind.

Part 2

A SOLUTION

Chapter 5

Reinventing the Commons

Imagination is more important than knowledge.
—Albert Einstein, 1929

Thus far I've argued that Capitalism 2.0—or surplus capitalism—has three tragic flaws: it devours nature, widens inequality, and fails to make us happier in the end. It behaves this way because it's programmed to do so. It *must* make thneeds, reward property owners disproportionately, and distract us from truer paths to happiness because its algorithms direct it to do so. Neither enlightened managers nor the occasional zealous regulator can make it behave much differently.

In this part of the book I advance a solution. The essence of it is to fix capitalism's operating system by adding a commons sector to balance the corporate sector. The new sector would supply virtuous feedback loops and proxies for unrepresented stakeholders: future generations, pollutees, and nonhuman species. And would offset the corporate sector's *negative* externalities with *positive* externalities of comparable magnitude. If the corporate sector devours nature, the commons sector would protect it. If the corporate sector widens inequality, the commons sector would reduce it. If the corporate

sector turns us into self-obsessed consumers, the commons sector
would reconnect us to nature, community, and culture. All this
would happen automatically once the commons sector is set up. The
result would be a balanced economy that gives us the best of both
sectors and the worst of neither.

To be sure, building an economic sector from scratch is a formidable task. Fortunately, the commons sector *needn't* be built from
scratch; it has an enormous potential asset base just waiting to be
claimed. That asset base is the commons itself, the gifts of nature
and society we inherit and create together. As we'll see, these gifts
are worth more than all private assets combined. It's the job of the
commons sector to organize and protect these gifts, and by so doing,
to save capitalism from itself.

Our Common Wealth

Everyone knows what *private* wealth is, even if they don't have much
of it. It's the property we inherit or accumulate individually, including fractional claims on corporations and mutual funds. In the
United States in 2005, this private wealth (minus mortgages and
other liabilities) totaled $48.5 trillion. As previously noted, the top
5 percent of Americans owns more of this treasure than the bottom
95 percent.

But there's another trove of wealth that's not so well-known:
our *common* wealth. Each of us is the joint recipient of a vast inheritance. This shared inheritance includes air and water, habitats and
ecosystems, languages and cultures, science and technologies, social
and political systems, and quite a bit more.

Common wealth is like the dark matter of the economic universe—it's everywhere, but we don't see it. One reason we don't see
it is that much of it is, literally, invisible. Who can spot the air, an

aquifer, or the social trust that underlies financial markets? The more relevant reason is our own blindness: the only economic matter we notice is the kind that glistens with dollar signs. We ignore common wealth because it lacks price tags and property rights.

I first began to appreciate common wealth when Working Assets launched its socially screened money market fund. My job was to write advertisements that spurred people to send us large sums of money. Our promise was that we'd make this money grow, without investing in really bad companies, and send it back—including the growth, but minus our management fee—any time the investor requested. It struck me as quite remarkable that people who didn't know us from a hole in the wall would send us substantial portions of their savings. Why, I wondered, did they trust us?

The answer, of course, was that they didn't trust *us,* they trusted *the system* in which we operated. They trusted that we'd prudently manage their savings not because we'd *personally* earned their confidence, but because they knew that if we didn't, the Securities and Exchange Commission or some district attorney would bust us. Beyond that, they trusted that the corporations we invested in were honest in computing their incomes and reliable in meeting their obligations. That trust, and the larger system it's based on, were built over generations, and we had nothing to do with it. In short, although Working Assets provided a service people willingly paid for, we also profited from a larger system we'd simply inherited.

I got another whiff of common wealth when Working Assets considered going public—that is, selling stock to strangers through an initial public offering. Our investment banker informed us that, simply by going public, we'd increase the value of our stock by 30 percent. He called this magic a *liquidity premium.* What he meant was that stock that can be sold in a market of millions is worth more than stock that has almost no market at all. This extra value would come not from anything *we* did, but from the socially created bonus of liquidity. We'd be reaping what others sowed. (In the end, we didn't go public because we didn't want to be subjected to Wall Street's calculus.)

Trust and liquidity, I eventually realized, are just two small rivulets in an enormous river of common wealth that encompasses nature, community, and culture. Nature's gifts are all those wondrous things, living and nonliving, that we inherit from the creation. Community includes the myriad threads, tangible and intangible, that connect us to other humans efficiently. Culture embodies our vast store of science, inventions, and art.

Despite its invisibility, the value of our common wealth is immense. How much, roughly, is it worth? It's easy to put a dollar value on private assets; they're traded regularly, so their exchange value—if not their intrinsic value—is readily knowable. This isn't the case with common wealth. Many shared inheritances are valuable beyond measure. Others are potentially quantifiable, but there's no current market for them.

Fortunately, economists are a clever lot, and they've developed methodologies to estimate the value of things that aren't traded. Using such methodologies, it's possible to get an order of magnitude for the value of common wealth. The conclusion that emerges from numerous studies is that even though much common wealth can't be valued monetarily, the parts that can be valued are worth more than all private assets combined (see figure 5.1).

It's worth noting that figure 5.1 understates the gap between common and private wealth. That's partly because it omits much common wealth that can't be quantified, and partly because a portion of the value attributed to private wealth is in fact an

Figure 5.1
APPROXIMATE VALUE OF COMMON, PRIVATE, AND STATE ASSETS, 2001 ($ TRILLIONS)

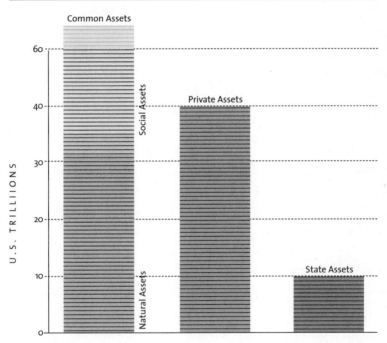

Reflects only quantifiable assets.
Source: Friends of the Commons, *State of the Commons 2003–04.*
http://friendsofthecommons.org/understanding/worth.html. Reprinted with permission.

appropriation of common wealth. If this mislabeled portion is sub-tracted from private wealth and added to common wealth, the gap between the two widens further.

An example may help explain this. Suppose you buy a house for $300,000, and without improving it, sell it a few years later for $400,000. You pay off the mortgage and walk away with a pile of cash. Your private wealth increases. But think about what *caused* the house to rise in value. It wasn't anything you did. Rather, it was the fact that your neighborhood became more popular. That, in turn,

HOW MUCH DO WE OWN?

Natural Assets

In 2002, economists Robert Costanza and Paul Sutton estimated the contribution of ecosystem services to the U.S. economy at $2 trillion. Ecosystem services represent the benefits humans derive from natural ecosystems, including food from wild plants and animals, climate regulation, waste assimilation, fresh water replenishment, soil formation, nutrient cycling, flood control, pollination, raw materials, and more. Using data from many previous studies, as well as satellite photography, Costanza and Sutton estimated values for ecosystems per unit of *biome* (an acre of rain forest, or grasslands, or desert, for example). They then multiplied by the total area of each biome and summed over all services and biomes.

If $2 trillion represents the yearly contribution of nature to the U.S. economy, what's the underlying value of America's natural assets? One way to answer this is to treat yearly ecosystem services as "earnings" produced by "stocks" of natural assets. These earnings can then be multiplied by the average price/earnings ratio of publicly traded stocks over the last fifty years (16.5/1) to arrive at an estimated natural asset value of $33 trillion.

This figure is, if anything, an underestimate, because it ignores a singular aspect of nature: its irreplaceability. If Corporation X were to go out of business, its useful contributions to society would quickly be supplied by another corporation. If a natural ecosystem were to disappear, however, it could not so easily be replaced. Thus, an *irreplaceability premium* of indeterminate magnitude should be added to the $33 trillion.

Social Assets

The value of community and cultural assets has been less studied than that of natural assets. However, we can get an order of magnitude by considering a few examples.

The Internet has contributed significantly to the U.S. economy since the 1990s. It has spawned many new companies (America Online, Amazon.com, Ebay, to name a few), boosted sales and efficiency of existing companies, and stimulated educational, cultural, and informational exchange. How much is all that worth?

There's no right answer to this question. However, a study by Cisco Systems and the University of Texas found that the Internet generated $830 billion in revenue in 2000. Assuming the asset value of the Internet is 16.5 times the yearly revenue it generates, we arrive at an estimated value of $13 trillion.

Another valuable social asset is the complex system of stock exchanges, laws, and communications media that makes it possible for Americans to sell stock easily. Assuming that this socially created "liquidity premium" accounts for 30 percent of stock market capitalization, its value in 2006 was roughly $5 trillion. If that much equity were put in a mutual fund whose shares belonged to all Americans, the average household would be $45,000 richer.

Not-for-profit cultural activities also pump billions of dollars into the U.S. economy. A 2002 study by Americans for the Arts found that nonprofit art and cultural activities generate $134 billion in economic value every year, including $89 billion in household income and $24 billion in tax revenues. Using the 16.5 multiplier suggests that America's cultural assets are worth in excess of $2 trillion.

These three examples alone add up to about $20 trillion. The long list of other social assets—including scientific and technical knowledge, our legal and political systems, our universities, libraries, accounting procedures, and transportation infrastructure—suggest that the total value of our social assets is comparable in magnitude to that of our natural assets.

resulted from population shifts, a new highway perhaps, an improved school, or the beautification efforts of neighbors. In other words, your increased wealth is a capture of socially created value. It shows up as private wealth but is really a gift of society.

These numbers, crude as they are, tell us something important. Despite our obsession with private wealth, most of what we cherish, we share. To believe otherwise is to imagine a flower's beauty owes nothing to nutrients in the soil, energy from the sun, or the activity of bees.

It's time to notice our shared gifts. Not only that, it's time to name them, protect them, and organize them. The practical question is *how?*

Common Property Is Property Too

In Dr. Seuss's *The Lorax,* the eponymous character speaks for the trees, while his antagonist, the Once-ler, speaks for industry, jobs, and growth. Though both characters use clever language, it's not an even match. The Once-ler has property rights, while the Lorax has only words. By the end of the story, the Once-ler has cut down all the truffula trees; the Lorax's protests are eloquent but futile. The obvious moral is: trees need property rights too.

And why not? Property rights are useful human inventions. They're legally enforceable agreements through which society grants specific privileges to owners. Among these are rights to use, exclude, sell, rent, lend, trade, or bequeath a particular asset. These assorted privileges can be bundled or unbundled almost any which way.

It's largely through property rights that economies are shaped. Feudal economies were based on estates passed from lords to their eldest sons, alongside commons that sustained the commoners. Commoners were required, in one way or another, to labor for the lords, while the lords lived off that labor and the bounty of the land. The whole edifice was anchored by the so-called divine right of kings.

Similarly, capitalism is shaped by the property rights we create and honor today. Its greatest invention has been the web of property rights we call the *joint stock corporation.* This fictitious entity enjoys perpetual life, limited liability, and—like the feudal estate of yester-year—almost total sovereignty. Its beneficial ownership has been fractionalized into tradeable shares, which themselves are a species of property.

There's nothing about property rights, however, that requires them to be concentrated in profit-maximizing hands. You could, for example, set up a trust to own a forest, or certain forest rights, on behalf of future generations. These property rights would talk as loudly as shares of Pacific Lumber stock, but their purpose would be very different: to preserve the forest rather than to exploit it. If the Lorax had owned some of these rights, Dr. Seuss's tale (and Pacific Lumber's) would have ended more happily.

Imagine a whole set of property rights like this. Let's call them, generically, *common property rights.* If such property rights didn't exist, there'd be a strong case for inventing them. Fortunately, they do exist in a variety of forms—for example, land or easements held in perpetual trust, as by the Nature Conservancy, and corporate assets managed on behalf of a broad community, as by the Alaska Permanent Fund.

Some forms of common property include individual shares— again, the Alaska Permanent Fund is an example. These individual shares, however, differ from shares in private corporations. They're not securities you can trade in a market; rather, they depend on your membership in the community. If you emigrate or die, you lose your share. Conversely, when you're born into the community, your share is a birthright.

I recognize that, for some, turning common wealth into *any* kind of property is a sacrilege. As Chief Seattle of the Suquamish tribe put it, "How can you buy or sell the sky, the warmth of the land?" I empathize deeply with this sentiment. However, I've come to believe that it's *more* disrespectful of the sky to pollute it without limit or payment than to turn it into common property held in trust for future generations. Hence, I favor *propertization,* but not privatization.

Organizing Principles of the Commons Sector

Property rights, especially the common kind, require competent institutions to manage them. What we need today, then, along with more common property, is a set of institutions, distinct from corporations and government, whose unique and explicit mission is to manage common property.

I say *set* of institutions because there will and should be variety. The commons sector should not be a monoculture like the corporate sector. Each institution should be appropriate to its particular asset and locale.

Some of the variety will depend on whether the underlying asset is limited or inexhaustible. Typically, gifts of nature have limited capacities; the air can safely absorb only so much carbon dioxide, the oceans only so many drift nets. Institutions that manage natural assets must therefore be capable of limiting use. By contrast, ideas and cultural creations have endless potential for elaboration and reuse. In these commons, managing institutions should maximize public access and minimize private tollbooths.

Despite their variations, commons sector institutions would share a set of organizing principles. Here are the main ones.

LEAVE ENOUGH AND AS GOOD IN COMMON

As Locke argued, it's okay to privatize *parts* of the commons as long as "enough and as good" is left for everyone forever. *Enough* in the case of an ecosystem means enough to keep it alive and healthy. That much, or more, should be part of the commons, even if parts of the ecosystem are private. In the case of culture and science, *enough* means enough to assure a vibrant public domain. Exclusive licenses, such as patents and copyrights, should be kept to a minimum.

PUT FUTURE GENERATIONS FIRST

Corporations put the interests of stockholders first, while government puts the interests of campaign donors and living voters first. No one at the moment puts future generations first. That's Job Number One for the commons sector.

In practice, this means trustees of common property should be legally accountable to future generations. (We'll see how this might work in chapter 6.) They should also be bound by the *precautionary principle*: when in doubt, err on the side of safety. And when faced with a conflict between short-term gain and long-term preservation, they should be required to choose the latter.

THE MORE THE MERRIER

Whereas private property is inherently *ex*clusive, common property strives to be *in*clusive. It always wants *more* co-owners or participants, consistent with preservation of the asset.

This organizing principle applies most clearly to commons like culture and the Internet, where physical limits are absent and increasing use unleashes synergies galore. It also applies to social compacts like Social Security and Medicare, which require universal participation. In these compacts, financial mechanisms express our solidarity with other members of our national community. They're efficient and fair because they include everybody. Were they to operate under profit-maximizing principles, they'd inevitably exclude the poor (who couldn't afford to participate) and anyone deemed by private insurers to be too risky.

ONE PERSON, ONE SHARE

Modern democratic government is grounded on the principle of one person, one vote. In the same way, the modern commons sector would be grounded on the principle of one person, one share.

In the case of scarce natural assets, it will be necessary to distinguish between usage rights and income rights. It's impossible for everyone to *use* a limited commons equally, but everyone should receive equal shares of the *income* derived from selling limited usage rights.

usage vs. income rights

INCLUDE SOME LIQUIDITY

Currently, private property owners enjoy a near-monopoly on the privilege of receiving property income. But as the Alaska Permanent Fund shows, it's possible for common property co-owners to receive income too.

Income sharing would end private property's monopoly not only on liquidity, but also on attention. People would *notice* common property if they got income from it. They'd care about it, think about it, and talk about it. Concern for invisible commons would soar.

Common property liquidity has to be designed carefully, though. Since common property rights are birthrights, they shouldn't be tradeable the way corporate shares are. This means commons owners wouldn't reap capital gains. Instead, they'd retain their shared income stakes throughout their lives, and through such stakes, share in rent, royalties, interest, and dividends.

A Glimpse Ahead

Unlike a computer operating system, Capitalism 3.0 won't come on a disk. It can't be downloaded, either. It must be built in the real world, asset by asset and commons by commons. The process is summed up in figure 5.2 and described more fully in chapter 9.

Under Capitalism 2.0, private corporations devour unorganized commons with help from the state. The playing field is heavily tilted. During the transition phase, the state assigns rights to commons institutions, just as it does to corporations. The playing field begins to level off. Finally, under Capitalism 3.0, private corporations and organized commons enhance and constrain each other. The state maintains a level playing field.

Figure 5.2
FROM HERE TO CAPITALISM 3.0

I: Capitalism 2.0

Private corporations
devour unorganized
commons with help
from the state.
The playing field is
heavily tilted.

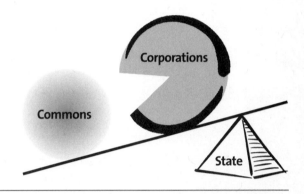

II: Reinventing the Commons

The state assigns
rights to commons
institutions, just as it
has to corporations.

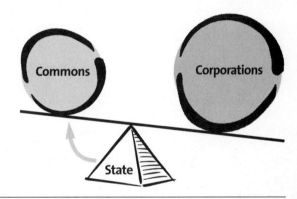

III: Capitalism 3.0

Private corporations
and organized
commons enhance
and constrain each
other. The state
maintains a level
playing field.

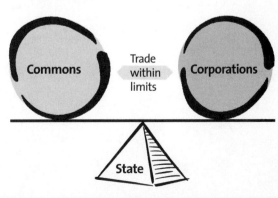

The next chapter takes a more detailed look at commons trusts and their economics, while the following two chapters explore culture and community.

Chapter 6

Trusteeship of Creation

God gave the care of his earth and its species to our first parents.
That responsibility has passed into our hands.
—**National Association of Evangelicals, 2004**

Gifts of creation were produced only once and are irreplaceable. By contrast, products traded in markets tend to be mass-produced and highly disposable. It's hard to imagine a deity who'd view such temporal goods as equivalent to his or her enduring handiwork. The question is whether creation's irreplaceable gifts are different enough to merit different treatment by our economic operating system. A strong case can be made that they are.

The case is moral as well as economic. The moral argument is that we have a duty to preserve irreplaceable gifts of creation, whereas we have no comparable duty toward transient commercial goods. The economic argument is that any society that depletes its natural capital is bound to become impoverished over time. I find both lines of argument convincing.

But what's the reality today? Here we encounter two disconcerting facts. The first is that there are very few property rights protecting nature's gifts. With the exception of a few set-asides such as parks and wilderness areas, we subject creation's gifts to the same rules as

Wal-Mart's merchandise. The second is that the right of corporations to profit dominates all other rights.

It's time to treat creation's gifts differently, to put different "tags" on them so markets will recognize them and apply different rules to them. This chapter shows how we can do that.

The Divine Right of Capital

The California drivers' handbook states: "At an intersection, yield to the car which arrives first or to the car on your right if it reaches the intersection at the same time you do." (I discovered this when my teenage son took his driving test.)

Why does the car on the right get priority over the car on the left? It's unclear. Quite possibly the rule is entirely arbitrary. But someone has to have the right of way or cars will collide. The same is true for boats at sea, and for moving objects in any complex system.

So too in a market economy. When two property rights come to the same intersection, one has to trump the other. Either capital can fire labor, or labor can fire capital. Either my right to pollute trumps your right not to be polluted, or vice versa. As they say in Hollywood, someone must get top billing.

But who? Marjorie Kelly has written a brilliant book called *The Divine Right of Capital.* By *divine* she doesn't mean God-given. She means that, under our current operating system, the rights of capital trump everything else. The rights of workers, communities, nature, and future generations—all play second fiddle to capital's prerogative to maximize short-term gain. This hierarchy isn't the doing of God or some inexorable law of nature. Rather, it's a result of political choice.

The question of who gets the top right in any society is always an interesting one. Invariably, the top dogs in any era assert that there's no alternative. Kings said it three hundred years ago; capital owners say it today. They hire priests and economists to add moral or pseudoscientific credence to their claims. The truth, though, is that societies choose their top right holders, and we can change our minds if we wish.

Kelly locates many places where capital's supremacy is written into our codes. Corporate directors, for example, are bound by law to put shareholders' financial gain first. If a raider offers a higher price for a publicly traded company than its current market value, directors have little choice but to sell, regardless of the consequences for workers, communities, or nature. Similarly, it's the fiduciary duty of mutual funds, pension funds, and other institutional investors to seek the highest returns for their shareholders or beneficiaries. This duty is embodied, among other places, in the Employee Retirement Income Security Act of 1974. Although the language of the act sounds innocent enough—a pension fund manager, like any trustee, "shall discharge his duties . . . solely in the interest of the participants and beneficiaries"—it results, ironically, in the financing of many workers' retirements by investing in companies that shift other workers' jobs overseas. Throw in the WTO and NAFTA, and the rights of capital stand comfortably astride everyone else's.

What's wrong here? It's not that businesses pursue profit; that's what they're designed to do and what we want them to do. The problem is that private capital rides in the front of the bus while everyone else rides in the back.

At the moment, there's one law that does give preference to creation's gifts: the Endangered Species Act, which says a species' right to survive trumps capital's right to short-term gain. The trouble is, the law comes into play only when a species has been so devastated it's on the brink of extinction. Even then, the courts don't always enforce it. Recently, in a very dry year, the government reduced its delivery of subsidized water to California farmers because endangered fish needed it to survive. Some farmers sued, arguing that the government had unconstitutionally "taken" their property. A federal court agreed, the Bush administration refused to appeal, and the farmers collected $13 million in damages.

It seems to me that, if anything is divine, it should be gifts of creation. Morally, they're gifts we inherit together and must pass on, undiminished, to future generations. Economically, they're irreplaceable and invaluable capital. Protection of these shared assets should trump transient private gain. Broad benefit should trump narrow benefit. The commons should trump capital. This should be written into our economic operating system and enforced by the courts.

From Gardens to Ecosystems

Trebah Garden is a spectacular piece of paradise in Cornwall, England, a ravine with a huge variety of trees and shrubs that winds its way down to a beach on the Helford River. Several years ago I visited this garden to enjoy its beauty. I soon learned that its history and governance are as interesting as its flora.

The property is first recorded in the *Domesday Book* of 1086 as belonging to the Bishop of Exeter. It passed through the hands of many squires and farmers until it was acquired in 1831 by a wealthy Quaker family, which developed the extraordinary garden. In the twentieth century the property changed hands several more times and the garden gradually deteriorated. The last private owners sank a small fortune into restoring the garden, then donated it to the Trebah Garden Trust, so it could be opened to the public and preserved for future generations.

Today, anyone can become a lifetime member of this trust by making a donation of £250. Members get free access to the garden (other visitors pay an admission fee) and elect a council to manage the property. They receive an annual report, audited accounts, and notices of meetings at which they may vote and submit resolutions. At present, there are about a thousand voting members of the trust.

As I wandered through the acres of ferns and rhododendrons, it struck me that Trebah is a microcosm for the ideas in this book. It has passed from private ownership to a form of common ownership that enables it to be shared and preserved. If we think of the world as an assemblage of gardens—that is, of ecosystems in which humans play active roles—the Trebah model becomes extremely interesting. It illuminates both a process by which natural gifts can shift from private to common ownership, and an institutional model—the trust—for managing such gifts as permanent parts of the commons.

Trusts are centuries-old institutions devised to hold and manage property for beneficiaries. The essence of a trust is a fiduciary relationship. Neither trusts nor their trustees may ever act in their own self-interest; they're legally obligated to act solely on behalf of beneficiaries.

Trusts are bound by numerous rules, including the following:

- Managers must act with undivided loyalty to beneficiaries.
- Unless authorized to act otherwise, managers must preserve the corpus of the trust. It's okay to spend income, but not to diminish principal.
- Managers must ensure transparency by making timely financial information available to beneficiaries.

These rules are enforceable. The basic enforcement mechanism is that an aggrieved beneficiary or a state attorney general can bring suit against a trustee. When that happens, the trustee must prove she acted prudently; if there's any doubt, the trustee is fined or fired. As Supreme Court Justice Benjamin Cardozo once put it: "A trustee is held to something stricter than the morals of the marketplace. Not honesty alone, but the punctilio of an honor the most sensitive, is the standard of behavior."

A trustee isn't the same thing as a steward. Stewards care for an asset, but their obligations are voluntary and vague. By contrast, trustees' obligations are mandatory and quite specific. Trusteeship is thus a more formal and rigorous responsibility than stewardship.

Trusts can be in charge of financial as well as physical assets. In this chapter, my concern is natural assets—gifts we inherit from creation. One of my premises is that each generation has a contract to pass on such gifts, undiminished, to those not yet born. If we are to keep this contract, *someone* must act as trustee of nature's gifts, or at least of the most endangered of them. The question is, who?

The candidates are government, corporations, and trusts. I argued earlier that neither corporations nor government can fulfill this function; they're both too bound to short-term private interests. That leaves trusts.

Common Property Trusts

The Trebah Garden Trust isn't a rarity. Across Britain, the National Trust—a nongovernmental charity founded in 1895—owns over six hundred thousand acres of countryside, six hundred miles of coastline, and two hundred historic buildings and gardens. It has over three million members who elect half of its fifty-two-person governing council (the other half are appointed by nonprofit organizations that share the trust's goals). In the United States, there are now over fifteen hundred Trebah-like trusts, protecting over nine million acres. On top of that, the fifty-five-year-old Nature Conservancy protects more than fifteen million acres.

Let's posit, then, a generic institution, the *common property trust*. It's a special kind of trust that manages assets that come from the commons and are meant to be preserved *as* commons. Common property trusts manage these assets first and foremost on behalf of future generations. They may have secondary beneficiaries, such as public education or residents of a particular locale, but such living beneficiaries take backseats to the yet-to-be-born. These trusts carry out their missions by owning and managing bundles of property rights. Here are two examples from my own backyard: the Marin Agricultural Land Trust (MALT) and the Pacific Forest Trust (PFT).

The demise of family farms and the loss of open space around cities are seemingly unstoppable trends. Yet in Marin County, just north of San Francisco, family-owned dairy, sheep, and cattle ranches have survived. A big reason is that ranchers there have an option: selling conservation easements to MALT.

A conservation easement is a voluntary agreement between a landowner and a trust that permanently limits uses of the land. The owner continues to own and use the land and may sell it or pass it on to her heirs. However, the owner gives up some of the rights associated with the land—for example, the right to build additional houses on it or to clear-cut trees. The trust that acquires the easement makes sure its terms are followed by the current as well as future owners.

In Marin County, MALT has preserved nearly forty thousand acres of farmland by buying conservation easements from ranchers. This represents about a third of the land currently farmed. The ranchers receive the difference between what the land would be worth if developed and what it's worth as a working farm. In effect, they're paid to be land stewards and to forgo future capital gains.

Most of MALT's money comes from public sources. What the public receives isn't an old-fashioned commons of shared pasturage, but a lasting pastoral landscape and a viable agricultural economy. That's not a bad alternative to suburban sprawl.

In much the same way, the Pacific Forest Trust acquires what it calls *working forest conservation easements* from private woodlands owners. Some of the easements are purchased, others are donated by owners in exchange for tax benefits. Here again, owners keep their land but agree to forgo nonforest development and to harvest trees sustainably.

PFT's goal is to protect not only forests themselves but the many species that live in them, as well as the ecosystem services— such as clean water and carbon absorption—that forests provide. As with MALT, some of PFT's money comes from public sources. In return, the public gets healthy forests for considerably less than it would cost to buy and manage them outright.

Valves and Their Keepers

One job of common property trusts is to preserve habitat and land-scapes, but such trusts can also play another role—controlling the flow of pollution into ecosystems. In this case, what they'd be manag-ing isn't the ecosystems themselves, but human economic activity *around* the ecosystems. In that sense, they'd be more like the Federal Reserve than the Nature Conservancy.

Let me back up here a bit. When I was in college, my econom-ics professors talked of fiscal and monetary "levers" that wise policy-makers could use to fine-tune the economy. This was in the early 1960s, still the heyday of Keynesianism. I imagined an economic control room full of gauges and valves, staffed by tweedy academics. Handsome, brainy men (it was still mainly men in those days) would scan readouts, puff on their pipes, and twist a few dials. Others would murmur praise. All would remain calm.

As I grew older, I learned the world is more chaotic than that. In reality, there's no economic control room. There's only one big valve—the money supply—and one person (with a few helpers) who turns it: the chair of the Federal Reserve. That valve has *some* effect on economy activity—when it's loose, interest rates fall and economic activity perks up; when it's tight, interest rates rise and economic activity ebbs. But the Fed's valve doesn't control everything our economic engine does. In particular, it has little impact on the rate at which we pour pollutants into surrounding ecosystems. To address this problem, we need more valves.

Think, for example, about carbon. At present, our economic engine is emitting far too much carbon dioxide into the atmosphere; this is destabilizing the climate. We desperately need a valve that can crank the carbon flow down. Let's assume we can design and install such a valve. (I explained how this can be done in my previous book, *Who Owns the Sky?* It involves selling a limited quantity of "upstream" permits to companies that bring fossil fuels into the economy.) The question then is, who should control the valve?

Unfettered markets can't be given that responsibility; as we've seen, they have no ability to limit polluting. So we're left with two options: government or trusts. Government is a political creature; its time horizon is short, and future generations have no clout in it. Common property trusts, by contrast, are fiduciary institutions. They have long time horizons and a legal responsibility to future generations. Given the choice, I'd designate a common property trust to be keeper of the carbon valve, based on peer-reviewed advice from scientists. Its trustees could make hard decisions without committing political suicide. They might be appointed by the president, like governors of the Fed, but they wouldn't be obedient to him the way cabinet members are. Once appointed, they'd be legally accountable to future generations.

Now imagine a goodly number of valves at the local, regional, and national levels, not just for carbon (which requires only one national valve) but for a variety of pollutants. Imagine also that the valve keepers are trusts accountable to future generations. They'd have the power to reduce some of the negative externalities—the illth—that corporations shift to the commons. They'd also have the power to auction limited pollution rights to the highest bidders, and to divide the resulting income among commons owners. That's something neither the Fed nor the EPA can do.

These trusts would fundamentally change our economic operating system. What are now unpriced externalities would become property rights under accountable management. If a corporation wanted to pollute, it couldn't just do so; it would have to buy the rights from a commons trust. The price of pollution would go up; corporate illth creation would go down. Ecosystems would be protected for future generations. More income would flow to ordinary citizens. Nonhuman species would flourish; human inequality would diminish. And government wouldn't be enlarged—our economic engine would do these things on its own.

One final point about valves. It's not too critical where we set them initially. It's far more important to install them in the right places, and to put the right people in charge. Then *they* can adjust the settings.

A Second Set of Books

Mental models begin with assumptions. Most economists today assume there are only two kinds of property, private (that is, corporate or individual) and state. There are no shared assets, no inter- or intragenerational obligations, and no nonhumans other than those we eat.

Yet as we've seen, many things are missing here. The most obvious omission is the great economy of nature within which the human enterprise operates. We're borrowing prodigiously from that economy, but not recording the loans. Equally absent are future generations, from whom we're borrowing just as wantonly and surreptitiously.

In a proper bookkeeping system, every loan shows up on two balance sheets, the borrower's and the lender's. One entity's liability is another entity's asset. But this isn't true in contemporary economics. When the human economy grows, assets on corporate and individual balance sheets go up, but nowhere is there a debit. In fact, there aren't any accounts that *could* be debited. There's only good growth on one side of the ledger, and on the other, a void in which illth and debt accumulate, uncounted and unnoticed.

In recent years, economists have added a few bits to this stripped-down model. For example, they now recognize *public goods* and *ecosystem services* as contributors of economic value. *Public goods* are services like national defense, education, and flood control, which benefit everyone but can't easily be sold at a profit. Because markets don't adequately supply them, governments step in and do so. Economists sometimes debate whether the value of these public goods exceeds the "burden" they impose on taxpayers, but they don't see the expenditures as adding value to any account, or to any asset owned by anyone.

Similarly, many economists now recognize *ecosystem services* as valuable inputs to the economy. However, the ecosystems that produce these services have no owners or balance sheets. They're just *there,* floating in space, with no connection to humans. What I'm suggesting is that economists treat them *as if they were common property held in trust.* This simple supposition would not only put ecosystems on the books, enabling us to track them better; it would also pave the way to real-world property rights that actually protect those ecosystems.

Beyond Coase's Supposes

"Let us suppose," economist Ronald Coase wrote in 1960, "that a farmer and a cattle-raiser are operating on neighboring properties." He went on to suppose further that the cattle-raiser's animals wander onto the farmer's land and damage his crops. From this hypothetical starting point Coase examined the problem of externalities and proposed a solution—the creation of rights to pollute or not be polluted upon. Today, pollution rights are used throughout the world. In effect, Coase conjured into existence a class of property rights that didn't exist before, and his leap of imagination eventually reduced real pollution.

"Let us suppose" is a wonderful way for anyone, economists included, to begin thinking. It lets us adjust old assumptions and see what might happen. And it lets us imagine things that don't exist but *could,* and sometimes, because we imagined them, later *do.*

Coase supposed that a single polluter or his neighboring pollutee possessed a right to pollute or not be polluted upon. He further supposed that the transaction costs involved in negotiations between the two neighbors were negligible. He made these suppositions half a century ago, at a time when *aggregate pollution* wasn't planet-threatening, as it now is. Given today's altered reality, it might be worth updating Coase's suppositions to make them relevant to this aggregate problem. Here, in my mind, are the appropriate new suppositions:

• Instead of one polluter, there are many, and instead of one
  pollutee, there are millions—including many not yet born.

- The pollutees (including future generations) are collectively represented by trusts.
- The initial pollution rights are assigned by government to these trusts.
- In deciding how many pollution permits to sell, the trustees' duty isn't to maximize revenue but to preserve an ecosystem for future generations. The trusts therefore establish safe levels of pollution and gradually reduce the number of permits they sell until those levels are reached.
- Revenue from the sale of pollution permits is divided 50 percent for per capita dividends (like the Alaska Permanent Fund) and 50 percent for public goods such as education and ecological restoration.

If we make these suppositions, what then happens? We have, first of all, an economic model with a second set of books. Not all, but many externalities show up on these new ledgers. More importantly, we begin to imagine a world in which nature and future generations are represented in real-time transactions, corporations internalize previously externalized costs, prices of illth-causing goods rise, and everyone receives some property income.

Here's what such a world could look like:

- Degradation of key ecosystems is gradually reduced to sustainable levels because the trustees who set commons usage levels are accountable to future generations, not living shareholders or voters. When they fail to protect their beneficiaries, they are sued.
- Thanks to per capita dividends, income is recycled from overusers of key ecosystems to underusers, creating both incentives to conserve and greater equity.

- Clean energy and organic farming are competitive because prices of fossil fuels and agricultural chemicals are appropriately high.
- Investment in new technologies soars and new domestic jobs are created because higher fuel and waste disposal prices boost demand for clean energy and waste recycling systems.
- Public goods are enhanced by permit revenue.

What has happened here? We've gone from a realistic set of assumptions about how the world *is* — multiple polluters and pollutees, zero cost of pollution, dangerous cumulative levels of pollution—to a reasonable set of expectations about how the world *could be* if certain kinds of property rights are introduced. These property rights go beyond Coase's, but are entirely compatible with market principles. The results of this thought experiment show that the introduction of common property trusts can produce a significant and long-lasting shift in economic outcomes without further government intervention.

Commons Rent

It shouldn't be thought that the commons is, or ought to be, a money-free zone. In fact, an important subject for economists (and the rest of us) to understand is commons rent.

By this I don't mean the monthly check you send to a landlord. In economics, rent has a more precise meaning: it's *money paid because of scarcity.* If you're not an economist, that may sound puzzling, but consider this. A city has available a million apartments. In absolute terms, that means apartments aren't scarce. But the city is confined geographically and demand for apartments is intense. In this economic sense, apartments *are* scarce. Now think back to that check you pay your landlord, or the mortgage you pay the bank. Part of it represents the landlord's operating costs or the bank's cost of money, but part of it is pure rent—that is, money paid for scarcity. That's why New Yorkers and San Franciscans write such large checks to landlords and banks, while people in Nebraska don't.

Rent rises when an increase in demand bumps into a limit in supply. Rent due to such bumping isn't good or bad; it just *is*. We can (and should) debate the *distribution* of that rent, but the rent itself arises automatically. And it's important that it does so, because this helps the larger economy allocate scarce resources efficiently. Other methods of allocation are possible. We can distribute scarce things on a first come, first served basis, or by lottery, political power, seniority, or race. Experience has shown, though, that selling scarce resources in open markets is usually the best approach, and such selling inevitably creates rent.

Rent was of great interest to the early economists—Adam Smith, David Ricardo, and John Stuart Mill, among others—because it constituted most of the money earned by landowners, and land was then a major cost of production. The supply of land, these economists noted, is limited, but demand for it steadily increases. So, therefore, does its rent. Thus, landowners benefit from what Mill called the *unearned increment*—the rise in land value attributable not to any effort of the owner, but purely to a socially created increase in demand bumping into a limited supply of good land.

The underappreciated American economist Henry George went further. Seeing both the riches and the miseries of the Gilded Age, he asked a logical question: Why does poverty persist despite economic growth? The answer, he believed, was the appropriation of rent by landowners. Even as the economy grew, the property rights system and the scarcity of land diverted almost all the gains to a landowning minority. Whereas competition limited the gains of working people, nothing kept down the landowners' gains. As Mill had noted, the value of their land just kept rising. To fix the problem, George advocated a steep tax on land and the abolition of other taxes. His best-selling book *Progress and Poverty* catapulted him to fame in the 1880s, but mainstream economists never took him seriously.

By the twentieth century, economists had largely lost interest in rent; it seemed a trivial factor in wealth production compared to capital and labor. But the twenty-first century ecological crisis brings rent back to center-stage. Now it's not just land that's scarce, but clean water, undisturbed habitat, biological diversity, waste absorption capacity, and entire ecosystems.

This brings us back to common property rights. The definition and allocation of property rights are the primary factors in determining who pays whom for what. If, in the case of pollution rights, pollution rights are given free to past polluters, the rent from the polluted ecosystem will also go to them. That's because prices for pollution-laden products will rise as pollution is limited (remember, if demand is constant, a reduction in supply causes prices to go up), and those higher prices will flow to producers (which is to say, polluters). By contrast, if pollution rights are assigned to trusts representing pollutees and future generations, and if these trusts then *sell* these rights to polluters, the trusts rather than the polluters will capture the commons rent. If the trusts split this money between per capita dividends and expenditures on public goods, everyone benefits.

At this moment, based on pollution rights allocated so far, polluting corporations are getting most of the commons rent. But the case for trusts getting the rent in the future is compelling. If this is done, consumers will pay commons rent not to corporations or government, but to themselves as beneficiaries of commons trusts. Each citizen's dividend will be the same, but his payments will depend on his purchases of pollution-laden products. The more he pollutes, the more rent he'll pay. High polluters will get back less than they put in, while low polluters will get back more. The microeconomic incentives, in other words, will be perfect. (See figure 6.1.)

What's equally significant, though less obvious, is that the macroeconomic incentives will be perfect too. That is, it will be in everyone's interest to reduce the total level of pollution. Remember how rent for scarce things works: the lower the supply, the higher the rent. Now, imagine you're a trustee of an ecosystem, and leaving aside (for the sake of argument) your responsibility to preserve the asset for future generations, you want to increase dividends. Do you raise the number of pollution permits you sell, or lower it? The correct, if counterintuitive answer is: you lower the number of permits.

Figure 6.1
COMMONS RENT RECYCLING THROUGH TRUSTS

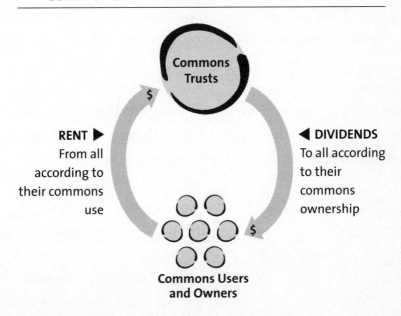

Commons Trusts

RENT ▶
From all according to their commons use

◀ DIVIDENDS
To all according to their commons ownership

Commons Users and Owners

Figure 6.2
WHEN LESS POLLUTION = MORE DIVIDENDS

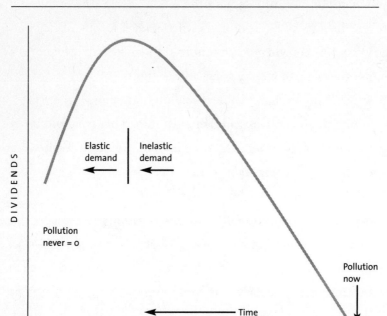

You crank down pollution—and wondrously, commons rent goes up. And so does everyone's dividend. (See figure 6.2.)

This macroeconomic phenomenon—that less pollution yields more income for citizens—is the ultimate knockout punch for commons trusts. It aligns the interests of future generations with, rather than against, those of living citizens. By so doing, it lets us chart a transition to sustainability in which the political pressure is for *faster* pollution reduction rather than slower.

There's one further argument for recycling commons rent through trusts. As rent is recycled from overusers of the commons to underusers, income is shifted from rich to poor. That's because rich households, on average, use the commons more than poor households. They drive SUVs, fly in jets, and have large homes to heat and cool—thus they dump more waste into the biosphere. Studies by Congress and independent economists have shown that only a rent recycling system like the one just described can protect the poor. Absent such a system, the poor will *pay* commons rent and get nothing back. In other words, they'll get poorer.

As always, there are a few caveats. First, to the extent commons rent is used for public goods rather than per capita dividends, the income recycling effects are diminished. This is offset, however, by the fact that public goods benefit everyone. Second, the less-pollution-equals-more-dividends formula doesn't work indefinitely. At some point after less polluting technologies have been widely deployed, the demand for pollution absorption will become elastic. Then, lowering the number of pollution permits sold will decrease income to citizens. But that time is far in the future, and when it comes, the world will be a healthier place. And even then, trustees won't be able to increase the number of pollution permits without violating their responsibility to future generations.

The Effect on Poverty

I'm now ready to make a bold assertion: *sharing commons rent through per capita dividends isn't just the best way to bring our economy into harmony with nature, it's also the best way to reduce poverty.* That's because there's no other pool of money of comparable size to which poor people have a legitimate claim.

The free market notion that those at the bottom of the ladder will somehow lift themselves out of poverty, without any capital or property, just isn't credible any longer. Our economic operating system has long been stacked against the poor, and globalization hasn't made it any less so. The prospects for taxing and spending the poor out of poverty aren't much brighter. Arguably, such policies reached their zenith in the Johnson era of the 1960s, and didn't get the job done.

The reason commons rent-sharing can work is that it's driven not only—or even primarily—by compassion for the poor. Rather, it's driven primarily by the need to preserve threatened ecosystems. When this problem is tackled, the question of who gets commons rent will necessarily arise; we can't solve the first problem without addressing the latter. We'll then have to decide whether to take, once again, the commons from the poor, or let them share in our joint inheritance.

The poor's claim on commons rent is, of course, no different from the claim of middle-income households or the rich: commons rent rightfully belongs to everyone. But commons rent, if fully paid, would boost living standards for the poor much more than for anyone else. And unlike other forms of help for the poor, commons rent can't be derided as welfare. It is, technically, unearned income, but no more so than dividends received by inheritors of private wealth. It's property income, and should be a universal property *right*. That, I believe, is a winnable political strategy, as well as sound economic policy.

Accountability and Democracy

The question I'm most often asked about commons trusteeship is: *How can we be sure trustees won't succumb to corporate influence, just as politicians have?* My answer is that, while there can be no guarantees, the odds of escaping corporate capture are much better with trustees than with elected officials.

The key reason is accountability. In the world of corporations, accountability is quite clear: directors must be loyal to shareholders. In the world of government, accountability is less clear. Elected officials must uphold the Constitution, but that's about it. If there are conflicts between workers and employers, polluters and pollutees, voters and donors, or future generations and current ones, whose side should politicians be on? There are no requirements or even guide-lines. Elected officials, as sovereign political actors, are free to do as they please.

The fact that politicians operate this way is no accident; it's what the Founders had in mind. The job of democratic government isn't to take, consistently, one side or another. Rather, it's to resolve disputes among factions peaceably, without trampling minorities. James Madison made this plain in the *Federalist Papers*. Voters can "fire" elected officials at regular intervals if a majority so chooses, but they can't expect loyalty to any particular constituency between elec-tions. It's this absence of built-in loyalty that opens the door to corpo-rate influence, a force the Founders didn't—and couldn't—foresee.

The decision-making of judges, it should be noted, isn't as untethered as that of legislators and executive officeholders. Their duty is to uphold not just the skeletal bones of the Constitution but the full flesh and blood of the law, with its thousands of pages and interpretations. They may, on occasion, interpret anew, but unless they're among a Supreme Court majority, all such reinterpretations are subject to review.

Trustees are in the same boat as judges, rather than the wide-open waters in which politicians swim. Their hands are constrained both by the law and by their fiduciary duty to beneficiaries. This isn't to say they have no room to wiggle: equally loyal trustees may differ over what's in the best interest of beneficiaries. Still, they are subject to court review, and they can't betray their beneficiaries too brazenly.

The tricky thing here is that the beneficiaries to whom we want commons trustees to be loyal—future generations, nonhumans, and ecosystems—are voiceless and powerless. We must therefore take extra care when we set up commons trusts. For example, we should install strict conflict-of-interest rules for trustees and managers. We should require that all relevant information about the trusts—including audited financial reports—are freely available on the Internet. We should ensure that, if a commons trust fails, its assets are transferred to a similar trust rather than privatized. We should build in internal watchdogs and ombudsmen. And we should authorize external advocates, such as nonprofit organizations, to represent nonliving beneficiaries who, by their very nature, can't take trustees to court. Most states assign this function to their attorneys general, but this is insufficient given the political pressures attorneys general are subject to.

With regard to the manner of selecting trustees, there's no single method. Trustees might be elected, appointed by outsiders, or be self-perpetuating like the boards of many nonprofits. This is as it should be; we don't live in a one-size-fits-all world. The important thing is that, once selected, trustees should have secure tenure, and—like judges—lengthy terms. Indeed, trustees should be like judges in other ways: professional, impeccably honest, well-compensated, and honored. Being a commons trustee should be a distinguished and attractive calling.

It might be argued that, by shielding trustees from direct political influence, we'd make them—and commons trusts generally—undemocratic. The same could be said, however, for our courts. The fact is, there are certain decisions, both economic and judicial, that *should* be shielded from politics and markets. Moreover, neither government nor corporations represent the needs of future generations, ecosystems, and nonhuman species. Commons trusts can do this. In that sense, they'd *expand* rather than constrict the boundaries of democracy.

Chapter 7

Universal Birthrights

We hold these truths to be self-evident, that all men are created equal,
that they are endowed by their Creator with certain unalienable Rights,
that among these are Life, Liberty and the pursuit of Happiness.
—U.S. Declaration of Independence, 1776

Capitalism and community aren't natural allies. Capitalism's emphasis on individual acquisition and consumption is usually antithetical to the needs of community. Where capitalism is about the pursuit of self-interest, community is about connecting to—and at times assisting—others. It's driven not by monetary gain but by caring, giving, and sharing.

While the opportunity to advance one's self-interest is essential to happiness, so too is community. No person is an island, and no one can truly attain happiness without connection to others. This raises the question of how to promote community. One view is that community can't be promoted; it either arises spontaneously or it doesn't. Another view is that community can be strengthened through public schools, farmers' markets, charitable gifts, and the like. It's rarely imagined that community can be built into our economic operating system. In this chapter I show how it can be—*if* our operating system includes a healthy commons sector.

The Rules of the Game

The perennially popular board game *Monopoly* is a reasonable simulacrum of capitalism. At the beginning of the game, players move around a commons and try to privatize as much as they can. The player who privatizes the most invariably wins.

But *Monopoly* has two features currently lacking in American capitalism: all players start with the same amount of capital, and all receive $200 each time they circle the board. Absent these features, the game would lack fairness and excitement, and few would choose to play it.

Imagine, for example, a twenty-player version of *Monopoly* in which one player starts with half the property. The player with half the property would win almost every time, and other players would fold almost immediately. Yet that, in a nutshell, is U.S. capitalism today: the top 5 percent of the population owns more property than the remaining 95 percent.

Now imagine, if you will, a set of rules for capitalism closer to the actual rules of *Monopoly.* In this version, every player receives, not an equal amount of start-up capital, but enough to choose among several decent careers. Every player also receives dividends once a year, and simple, affordable health insurance. This version of capitalism produces more happiness for more people than our current version, without ruining the game in any way. Indeed, by reducing lopsided starting conditions and relieving employers of health insurance costs, it makes our economy *more* competitive and productive.

If you doubt the preceding proposition, consider the economic operating systems of professional baseball, football, and basketball. Each league shifts money from the richest teams to the poorest, and gives losing teams first crack at new players. Even George Will, the conservative columnist, sees the logic in this: "The aim is not to guarantee teams equal revenues, but revenues sufficient to give each team periodic chances of winning if each uses its revenues intelligently." Absent such revenue sharing, Will explains, teams in twenty of the thirty major-league cities would have no chance of winning, fans would drift away, and even the wealthy teams would suffer. Too much inequality, in other words, is bad for everyone.

The Idea of Birthrights

John Locke's response to royalty's claim of divine right was the idea of everyone's inherent right to *life, liberty, and property.* Thomas Jefferson, in drafting America's Declaration of Independence, changed Locke's trinity to *life, liberty, and the pursuit of happiness.* These, Jefferson and his collaborators agreed, are gifts from the creator that can't be taken away. Put slightly differently, they're *universal birthrights.*

The Constitution and its amendments added meat to these elegant bones. They guaranteed such birthrights as free speech, due process, habeas corpus, speedy public trials, and secure homes and property. Wisely, the Ninth Amendment affirmed that "the enumeration in the Constitution, of certain rights, shall not be construed to deny or disparage others retained by the people." In that spirit, others have since been added.

If we were to analyze the expansion of American birthrights, we'd see a series of waves. The first wave consisted of rights against the state. The second included rights against unequal treatment based on race, nationality, gender, or sexual orientation. The third wave— which, historically speaking, is just beginning—consists of rights not *against* things, but *for* things—free public education, collective bargaining for wages, security in old age. They can be thought of as rights necessary for the pursuit of happiness.

What makes this latest wave of birthrights strengthen community is their universality. If some Americans could enjoy free public education while others couldn't, the resulting inequities would divide rather than unite us as a nation. The universality of these rights puts everyone in the same boat. It spreads risk, responsibility, opportunity, and reward across race, gender, economic classes, and generations. It makes us a nation rather than a collection of isolated individuals.

Universality is also what distinguishes the commons sector from the corporate sector. The starting condition for the corporate sector, as we've seen, is that the top 5 percent owns more shares than everyone else. The starting condition for the commons sector, by contrast, is one person, one share.

The standard argument against third wave universal birthrights is that, while they might be nice in theory, in practice they are too expensive. They impose an unbearable burden on "the economy"— that is, on the winners in unfettered markets. Much better, therefore, to let everyone—including poor children and the sick—fend for themselves. In fact, the opposite is often true: universal birthrights, as we'll see, can be cheaper and more efficient than individual acquisition. Moreover, they are always fairer.

How far we might go down the path of extending universal birthrights is anyone's guess, but we're now at the point where, economically speaking, we can afford to go farther. Without great difficulty, we could add three birthrights to our economic operating system: one would pay everyone a regular dividend, the second would give every child a start-up stake, and the third would reduce and share medical costs. Whether we add these birthrights or not isn't a matter of economic ability, but of attitude and politics.

Why attitude? Americans suffer from a number of confusions. We think it's "wrong" to give people "something for nothing," despite the fact that corporations take common wealth for nothing all the time. We believe the poor are poor and the rich are rich because they deserve to be, but don't consider that millions of Americans work two or three jobs and still can't make ends meet. Plus, we think tinkering with the "natural" distribution of income is "socialism," or "big government," or some other manifestation of evil, despite the fact that our current distribution of income isn't "natural" at all, but rigged from the get-go by maldistributed property.

The late John Rawls, one of America's leading philosophers, distinguished between *pre*distribution of property and *re*distribution of income. Under income *re*distribution, money is taken from "winners" and transferred to "losers." Understandably, this isn't popular with winners, who tend to control government and the media. Under property *pre*distribution, by contrast, the playing field is leveled by spreading property ownership *before* income is generated. After that, there's no need for income redistribution; property itself distributes income to all. According to Rawls, while income *re*distribution creates dependency, property *pre*distribution empowers.

But how can we spread property ownership without taking property from some and giving it to others? The answer lies in the commons—wealth that already belongs to everyone. By propertizing (without privatizing) some of that wealth, we can make everyone a property owner.

What's interesting is that, for purely ecological reasons, we *need* to propertize (without privatizing) some natural wealth now. This twenty-first century necessity means we have a chance to save the planet, and as a bonus, add a universal birthright.

Dividends from Common Assets

A cushion of reliable income is a wonderful thing. It can be saved for rainy days or used to pursue happiness on sunny days. It can encourage people to take risks, care for friends and relatives, or volunteer for community service. For low-income families, it can pay for basic necessities.

Conversely, the absence of reliable income is a terrible thing. It heightens anxiety and fear. It diminishes our ability to cope with crises and transitions. It traps many families on the knife's edge of poverty, and makes it harder for the poor to rise.

So why don't we, as *Monopoly* does, pay everyone some regular income—not through redistribution of income, but through predistribution of common property? One state—Alaska—already does this. As noted earlier, the Alaska Permanent Fund uses revenue from state oil leases to invest in stocks, bonds, and similar assets, and from those investments pays yearly dividends to every resident. Alaska's model can be extended to any state or nation, whether or not they have oil. We could, for instance, have an *American* Permanent Fund that pays equal dividends to long-term residents of all 50 states. The reason is, we jointly own many valuable assets.

Recall our discussion about common property trusts. These trusts could crank down pollution and earn money from selling ever-scarcer pollution permits. The scarcer the permits get, the higher their prices would go. Less pollution would equal more revenue. Over time, trillions of dollars could flow into an American Permanent Fund.

What could we do with that common income? In Alaska the deal with oil revenue is 75 percent to government and 25 percent to citizens. For an American Permanent Fund, I'd favor a 50/50 split, because paying dividends to citizens is so important. Also, when scarce ecosystems are priced above zero, the cost of living will go up and people will need compensation; this wasn't, and isn't, the case in Alaska. I'd also favor earmarking the government's dollars for specific public goods, rather than tossing them into the general treasury. This not only ensures identifiable public benefits; it also creates constituencies who'll defend the revenue sharing system.

Waste absorption isn't the only common resource an American Permanent Fund could tap. Consider also, the substantial contribution society makes to stock market values. As noted earlier, private corporations can inflate their value dramatically by selling shares on a regulated stock exchange. The extra value derives from the enlarged market of investors who can now buy the corporation's shares. Given a total stock market valuation of about $15 trillion, this socially created liquidity premium is worth roughly $5 trillion.

At the moment, this $5 trillion gift flows mostly to the 5 percent of the population that own more than half the private wealth. But if we wanted to, we could spread it around. We could do that by charging corporations for using the public trading system, just as investment bankers do. (For those of you who haven't been involved in a public stock offering, investment bankers are like fancy doormen to a free palace. While the public charges almost nothing to use the capital markets, investment bankers exact hefty fees.)

The public's fee could be in cash or stock. Let's say we required publicly traded companies to deposit 1 percent of their shares each year in the American Permanent Fund for ten years—reaching a total of 10 percent of their shares. This would be our price not just for using a regulated stock exchange, but also for all the other privileges (limited liability, perpetual life, copyrights and patents, and so on) that we currently bestow on private corporations for free.

In due time, the American Permanent Fund would have a diversified portfolio worth several trillion dollars. Like its Alaskan counterpart, it would pay equal yearly dividends to everyone. As the stock market rose and fell, so would everyone's dividend checks. A rising tide would lift all boats. America would truly be an "ownership society."

A Children's Opportunity Trust

Not long ago, while researching historic documents for this book, I stumbled across this sentence in the Northwest Ordinance of 1787: "[T]he estates, both of resident and nonresident proprietors in the said territory, dying intestate, shall descent to, and be distributed among their children, and the descendants of a deceased child, in equal parts." What, I wondered, was this about?

The answer, I soon learned, was *primogeniture*—or more precisely, ending primogeniture in America. Jefferson, Madison, and other early settlers believed the feudal practice of passing all or most property from father to eldest son had no place in the New World. This wasn't about equal rights for women; that notion didn't arise until later. Rather, it was about leveling the economic playing and avoiding a permanent aristocracy.

A nation in which everyone owned some property—in those days, this meant land—was what Jefferson and his contemporaries had in mind. In such a society, hard work and merit would be rewarded, while inherited privilege would be curbed. This vision of America wasn't wild romanticism; it seemed quite achievable at the time, given the vast western frontier. What thwarted it, later, were giveaways of land to speculators and railroads, the rise of monopolies, and the colossal untaxed fortunes of the robber barons.

Fast-forward to the twenty-first century. Land is no longer the basis for most wealth; stock ownership is. But Jefferson's vision of an ownership society is still achievable. The means for achieving it lies not, as George W. Bush has misleadingly argued, in the privatization of Social Security and health insurance, but in guaranteeing an inheritance to every child. In a country as super-affluent as ours, there's absolutely no reason why we can't do that. (In fact, Great Britain has already done it. Every British child born after 2002 gets a trust fund seeded by $440 from the government—$880 for children in the poorest 40 percent of families. All interest earned by the trust funds is tax-free.)

Let me get personal for a minute. My parents weren't wealthy; both were children of penniless immigrants. They worked hard, saved, and invested—and paid my full tuition at Harvard. Later, they helped me buy a home and start a business. Without their financial assistance, I wouldn't have achieved the success that I have. I, in turn, have set up trust funds for my two sons. As I did, they'll have money for college educations, buying their own homes, and if they choose, starting their own businesses—in other words, what they need to get ahead in a capitalist system.

As I hope my sons will be, I'm extremely grateful for my economic good fortune. At the same time, I'm painfully aware that my family's good fortune is far from universal. Many second-, third-, and even seventh-generation Americans have little or no savings to pass on to their heirs. Their children may receive their parents' love and tutelage, but they don't get the cash needed nowadays for a first-rate education, a down payment on a house, or a business venture. A few may rise because of extraordinary talent and luck, but the majority will spend their lives on a treadmill, paying bills and perhaps tucking a little away for old age. Their sons and daughters, in turn, will face a similar future.

It doesn't have to be this way. One can imagine all sorts of government programs that can help people advance in life—free college and graduate school, GI bills, housing subsidies, and so on. Such programs, as we know, come and go, and I prefer more rather than less of them. But the simplest way to help people advance is to give them what my parents gave me, and what I'm giving my sons: a cash inheritance. And the surest way to do that is to build such inheritances into our economic operating system, much the way Social Security is.

When Jefferson substituted *pursuit of happiness* for Locke's *property,* he wasn't denigrating the importance of property. Without presuming to read his mind, I assume he altered Locke's wording to make the point that property isn't an end in itself, but merely a means to the higher end of happiness. In fact, the importance he and other Founders placed on property can be seen throughout the Constitution and its early amendments. Happiness, they evidently thought, may be the ultimate goal, but property is darn useful in the pursuit of it.

If this was true in the eighteenth century, it's even truer in the twenty-first. The unalienable right to pursue happiness is fairly meaningless under capitalism without a chunk of capital to get started. And while Social Security provides a cushion for the back end of life, it does nothing for the front end. That's where we need something new.

A kitty for the front end of life has to be financed differently than Social Security because children can't contribute in advance to their own inheritances. But the same principle of intergenerational solidarity can apply. Consider an intergenerational transfer fund through which departing souls leave money not just for their own children, but for *all* children. This could replace the current inheritance tax, which is under assault in any case. (As this is written, Congress has temporarily phased out the inheritance tax as of 2010; a move is afoot to make the phaseout permanent.) Mind you, I think ending the inheritance tax is a terrible idea; it's the least distorting (in the sense of discouraging economic activity) and most progressive tax possible. It also seems sadly ironic that a nation that began by abolishing primogeniture is now on the verge of creating a permanent aristocracy of wealth. That said, if the inheritance tax *is* eliminated, an intergenerational transfer fund would be a fitting substitute.

The basic idea is similar to the revenue recycling system of professional sports. Winners—that is, millionaires and billionaires— would put money into a kitty (call it the Children's Opportunity Trust), to be divided among all children equally, so the next round of economic play can be more competitive. In this case, the winners will have had a lifetime to enjoy their wealth, rather than just a single season. When they depart, half their estates, say, could be passed to their own children, while the other half would be distributed among all children. Their own offspring would still start on third base, but others would at least be in the game.

Under this plan, no money would go to the government. Instead, every penny would go back into the market, through the bank or brokerage accounts (managed by parents) of newborn children. I'd call these new accounts Individual Inheritance Accounts; they'd be front-of-life counterparts of Individual Retirement Accounts. After children turn eighteen, they could withdraw from their accounts for further education, a first home purchase, or to start a business.

Yes, contributions to the Children's Opportunity Trust would be mandatory, at least for estates over a certain size (say $1 or $2 million). But such end-of-life gifts to society are entirely appropriate, given that so much of a millionaire's wealth is, in reality, a gift *from* society. No one has expressed this better than Bill Gates Sr., father of the world's richest person. "We live in a place which is orderly. It's a place where markets work because there's legal structure to support them. It's a place where people can own property and protect it. People who have the good fortune, the skill, the luck to become wealthy in our country, simply have a debt to the source of their opportunity."

I like the link between end-of-life recycling and start-of-life inheritances because it so nicely connects the passing of one generation with the coming of another. It also connects those who have received much from society with those who have received little; there's justice as well as symmetry in that.

To top things off, I like to think that the contributors—millionaires and billionaires all—will feel less resentful about repaying their debts to society if their repayments go directly to children, rather than to the Internal Revenue Service. They might think of the Children's Opportunity Trust as a kind of venture capital fund that makes startup investments in American children. A venture capital fund assumes nine out of ten investments won't pay back, but the tenth will pay back in spades, more than compensating for the losers. So with the Children's Opportunity Trust. If one out of ten children eventually departs this world with an estate large enough to "pay back" in spades the initial investment, then the trust will have earned its keep. And who knows? Some of those paying back might even feel good about it.

Health Risk Sharing

Pooled risk sharing, or social insurance, has several advantages over individualized risk. One is universality: everyone is covered and assured a dignified existence. Another is fairness: when risks are individualized, some people fare well, but others do not. There are winners and losers, and the disparities can be great.

Social insurance principles have been applied in America to the risks of old-age poverty, temporary unemployment, and disability. In every other capitalist democracy, they've been applied to these risks *and* ill health. The United States provides universal health insurance only to people age sixty-five and older. Extending this coverage to all Americans would be another pillar of the commons sector and make us more of a national community.

For the benefit of U.S. readers, it's worth describing how universal health insurance works. Take our northern neighbor as a case in point. In 1984, the Canadian Parliament unanimously passed the Canada Health Act, designed to ensure that all residents of Canada have access to necessary hospital and physician services on a prepaid basis. Each province now runs its own insurance program in accordance with five federal principles:

- *Universal.* All residents are covered.
- *Comprehensive.* All medically necessary services are covered.
- *Not-for-profit.* Each provincial plan is not-for-profit.
- *Accessible.* Premiums are affordable or subsidized.
- *Portable.* Coverage continues when a person travels.

The act also bans extra billing by medical practitioners. As a result, the system is incredibly simple. For routine doctor visits, Canadians need only present their health card. There are no forms to fill out or bills to pay. The system is financed by a combination of federal and provincial funds. The provinces raise part of their funds by charging monthly premiums.

I compared monthly premiums in 2005 for families of four in California (through Aetna) and in British Columbia (through the provincial health plan). For the California family, the rate was $1,045 when the head of household is age forty-five; for the Canadian family, the rate was $88 no matter what the age of the parents (see figure 7.1). Discounts are available to low-income families.

It's important to note that in Canada, unlike Britain, there's no National Health Service. Medical providers work for themselves, or for private clinics and hospitals. Customers can freely choose their doctors, hospitals, and other practitioners. The only thing that's been added to the commons is the risk-sharing system.

Here's the bottom line. All Canadians get health care and peace of mind at a per capita cost that's about 45 percent lower than ours. Canada lays out less than ten cents of every health care dollar on administration, while we spend nearly thirty cents (and that doesn't include the time and energy patients themselves spend on paperwork). What's more, our health care system doesn't even keep us healthy. Our infant mortality rate is higher than Canada's, our life expectancy is lower, and we have proportionally more obesity, cancer, diabetes, and depression. To top it off, forty-five million of us have no health insurance at all.

What can we learn from this comparison? Social insurance enables members of a community to reduce common risks more

Figure 7.1
HEALTH CARE BY THE NUMBERS: UNITED STATES AND CANADA

	U.S.	CANADA
Estimated per capita expenditures (2004; US$)	$6,040	$3,326
Percent spent on administration (1999)	26%	10%
Monthly premium for a family of four	$1,045	$88
Male life expectancy (years)	75	77
Female life expectancy (years)	81	84
Infant mortality (per 1,000 births)	6.4	4.7

cheaply and efficiently than private insurance does. It's thus a vital piece of social infrastructure. This is especially so when we want coverage to be universal. Some of the savings result from economies of scale and low marketing and administrative costs. Others result from simplicity and the absence of profit.

ARGUMENTS AND COUNTERARGUMENTS
FOR UNIVERSAL DIVIDENDS

Argument: Paying dividends to everyone would undermine the work ethic.

Counterargument: This might be true if the dividends were very high, but is unlikely to be true if they're kept at a modest level. Such dividends would supplement, but not replace, labor income. At the same time, they'd give people a little more freedom to take time off or to engage in uncompensated work at home or in their communities. Actually, a case can be made *for* slightly reducing the work ethic. With ever more jobs moving overseas, it's by no means certain we can keep all Americans employed. If some people *choose* to work less, that might be a good thing.

Argument: Paying people "something for nothing" would hurt the economy.

Counterargument: Our economy already pays many people for doing nothing, or for doing fairly useless things; it also overpays people who do useful things. None of this really hurts the economy as long as people spend or invest the money they're paid. In fact, paying people for "nothing" could actually help our economy, once we recognize that there's more to the economy than what shows up in gross domestic product. If people had a small cushion of nonlabor income, many would go back to school, start small businesses, spend more time with their kids, pursue artistic impulses, or participate in community life. All these activities would add to our nation's well-being.

Argument: Charging higher prices for nature's products would lower our living standards.

Counterargument: It's true that prices of many things, including gasoline and electricity, would rise, and this would compel many people—especially poor people—to consume less of these things. However, these price rises would be offset by dividends; many people would come out ahead. There could also be hardship grants, and grants to help people insulate their homes. Eventually, new technologies friendly to nature would replace current technologies, and living standards would be preserved if not improved.

Chapter 8

Sharing Culture

He who receives an idea from me, receives instruction himself
without lessening mine, as he who lights his taper at mine,
receives light without darkening me.
—Thomas Jefferson, 1813

So far I've focused on the commons of nature and community. In this chapter I explore the third fork of the commons river, culture. By this I mean the gifts of language, art, and science we inherit, plus the contributions we make as we live.

Culture is a joint undertaking—a co-production—of individuals and society. The symphonies of Mozart, like the songs of Lennon and McCartney, are works of genius. But they also arise from the culture in which that genius lives. The instrumentation, the notation system, and the prevalent musical forms are the dough from which composers bake their cakes. So too with ideas. All thinkers and writers draw on stories and discoveries that have been developed by countless men and women before them. To paraphrase Isaac Newton, each generation sees a little farther because it stands on the shoulders of its predecessors. In this way, all new work draws from the commons and then enriches it. To keep art and science flourishing, we have to make sure the cultural commons is cared for.

In addition, unlike most natural commons, the cultural commons is inexhaustible. Shakespeare's plays can be "used" again and again without diminishing them. The same is true of Newton's theories, Beethoven's string quartets, and the information on the World Wide Web. Indeed, the more we use these assets, the more value they bestow. And thanks to technology—from Gutenberg's press to Marconi's radio to the globe-spanning Internet—sharing this wealth has become increasingly easy.

Today, unfortunately, this cultural commons, like the commons of nature and community, is being enclosed by private corporations. The danger is that corporations will deplete the soil in which culture grows. The remedy is to reinvigorate the cultural commons.

Paying Our Pipers

Artists and scientists need to eat. In the past, wealthy private patrons supported them. They still do today, as do government and universities, but the sum of their gifts is insufficient. So where can additional money come from? The answers affect not just the quantity of art and science, but the quality.

Consider literature first. Prior to Gutenberg, books were copied by hand, mostly by monks, and there weren't many of them (books, that is). As printing spread, authors sold their writings to printers for a flat fee. Printers sold as many copies as they could, and kept the proceeds.

The Statute of Queen Anne, passed by the English Parliament in 1710, gave authors, not printers, title to their works. Such title was in the form of an exclusive right for fourteen years, with an option to renew for the same period. Thereafter, works would enter what we now call the *public domain,* and anyone could reprint them without further compensating the author. The idea was to reward authors sufficiently to induce them to write, but once they'd been fairly paid, to have literature circulate as widely and as cheaply as possible.

A leading advocate of this new arrangement was John Locke. As with landed property, Locke sought to balance the interest of the laborer who adds value with that of the commons that stores and shares value. In a memorandum to Parliament, he argued that it was "unreasonable and injurious to learning" to grant exclusive rights to print classic texts; the "liberty, to any one, of printing them, is certainly the way to have them the cheaper and the better." As for "authors that now live and write," he proposed "to limit their property to a certain number of years after . . . the first printing of the book."

In this spirit, the U.S. Constitution gave Congress authority "to promote the Progress of Science and useful Arts, by securing for limited Times to Authors and Inventors the exclusive Right to their respective Writings and Discoveries." Shortly thereafter, in 1790, the first American copyright law gave authors the same deal as in Britain: exclusive rights for fourteen years, with an option to renew for another fourteen. After that, their work entered the public domain. The idea wasn't so much to expand intellectual property rights as to set boundaries on them. Indeed, what we call *intellectual property* today was then considered a monopoly privilege granted by the state, not a right belonging to a creator.

For nearly two centuries, this arrangement worked brilliantly. There was no lack of creativity on either side of the Atlantic. But starting about thirty years ago, large entertainment companies began tipping the balance from the public domain to the private. Led by the Walt Disney Company, the corporations pushed Congress to extend copyright terms, first to seventy-five years and then to ninety-five. (The extensions occurred whenever Mickey Mouse was about to enter the public domain.) One consequence is that the public domain has been marginalized; corporations now take from the commons and give nothing back. Another is that the experience of culture has been altered; we're now consumers of culture rather than participants.

This isn't to say that corporate art is bad art; much of what Hollywood produces is astonishingly good. The trouble is that, with its massive advertising and distribution budgets, it tends to overwhelm local and live art. There's more intimacy, spontaneity, and experimentation in this kind of art. Local art also builds community, not only among artists but among audience members too. The challenge is to have both this kind of art *and* corporate art.

One can imagine a culture in which free concerts in parks, poets in schools and libraries, independent theaters and filmmakers, and murals and sculptures by local artists in public spaces thrive alongside corporate entertainment. There's no lack of artists who'd participate in such a culture, or of nonartists who'd appreciate it. The problem is how to pay for it.

What we need is a parallel economy for noncorporate art. Fortunately, models of such an economy exist. For example, there's the San Francisco Grants for the Arts program, funded from a tax on hotel rooms. Since 1961, the program has distributed over $145 million to hundreds of nonprofit cultural organizations. It's a prime

DISNEY STORIES TAKEN FROM THE PUBLIC DOMAIN

Aladdin
Atlantis
Beauty and the Beast
Cinderella
Davy Crockett
The Legend of Sleepy Hollow
Hercules
The Hunchback of Notre Dame
The Jungle Book
Oliver Twist
Pinocchio
Robin Hood
Snow White
Sleeping Beauty
The Three Musketeers
Treasure Island
The Wind in the Willows

DISNEY STORIES ADDED TO THE PUBLIC DOMAIN

None

reason the city pulses with free concerts, murals, film festivals, and theater in the park.

Then there's the Music Performance Trust Fund, set up in 1948. To settle a dispute with the musicians' union, the recording industry agreed to pay a small royalty from recording sales into a fund supporting live concerts in parks, schools, and other public venues. The fund was, and continues to be, administered by an independent trustee. In 2004 it sponsored over eleven thousand free concerts throughout the United States and Canada. Thanks to this system, sales of corporate-owned music support the living culture on which the recording industry ultimately depends.

These models could be scaled up. As a revenue source, consider what companies like Disney get with their copyrights. They get ninety-five-year protection for their movies, they get those FBI warnings on our DVDs, they get the U.S. government extending intellectual property rights worldwide, and they get police busting street vendors for selling "pirated" DVDs. That kind of protection is worth big bucks. Yet the companies' price tag for it is exactly zero. (They do pay taxes, but so does everybody else.)

What if, instead of supplying copyright protection for free, we charged a royalty on sales of electronically reproduced music, films, and video games? This could be supplemented by charging broadcasters for their exclusive licenses, and advertisers for their invasions of our brains (see the following section). The resulting billions could be distributed, through a National Arts Trust, to local arts councils, which in turn would support community arts institutions and artists.

Under this system, corporations would give back to a commons they now take from for free. More art would be live and local, and more artists would be employed. We'd have corporate *and* authentic culture at the same time.

What to Do About Advertising

Mind-time is precious to me. I resent it when random outsiders, trying to sell thneeds, get inside my brain. I resent it even more when they get inside my children's brains. What they claim is free speech, I experience as mental trespassing, and so do millions of others. As Kalle Lasn has written, "Our mental environment is a commons like air or water. We need to protect it from unwanted incursions."

Advertising—and by this I mean all forms of commercial attention-seeking—is part of the dark side of surplus capitalism. (I say this as one who, during my own career, modestly added to the din.) It's one of those borderline activities that's necessary, or at least acceptable, in moderation, but becomes dangerous when it spirals out of control. The trouble is that advertising escalates inexorably. Every new product needs to announce itself. Moreover, the greater the ambient noise, the more each ad has to shout in order to be heard. If anything is a "tragedy of the commons," this is it (though here, again, the commons is victim, not cause).

Here are a few statistics that confirm what everyone knows. Children in America see, on average, one hundred thousand television ads by age five; before they die they'll see another two million. In 2002, marketers unleashed eighty-seven billion pieces of junk mail, fifty-one billion telemarketing calls, and eighty-four billion pieces of email spam. In 2004, a Yankelovich poll found that 65 percent of Americans "feel constantly bombarded with too much advertising and marketing."

Advertising isn't just an occasional trespass of one person against another; it's a continuous trespass of relatively few corporations (the one hundred or so that do the most advertising) against all the rest of us. These companies want to—indeed *have* to—increase their sales, and for this they need access to our minds. But mind-time is a scarce resource. We have only so many hours of it a day, and so many days in our lives. Because of this scarcity, every neuro-minute occupied by an ad is one less neuro-minute available for our own thoughts and feelings. Every ad thus has an opportunity cost, a cost we experience but advertisers don't pay.

Ads also have other side effects. They bias us to high-priced branded products, to junk foods rather than healthy foods, and to spending rather than saving. They diminish our self-esteem by suggesting that we never have enough or look good enough. And ultimately, they diminish our natural wealth by increasing pollution and depleting resources.

As individuals, we can do a few things to protect ourselves against ads: we can turn off our television, delete email spam, and toss junk mail in the recycling bin. But that doesn't dampen the collective noise, or do much to reduce the external costs of ads. To do that we need economy-wide volume controls.

At present, there are no such controls. Though the airwaves belong to the people, no public agency limits TV advertising time. Until 1982, the major networks adhered to a voluntary code limiting ads to 9.5 minutes per hour in prime time. Then, profit maximizing took over, and the networks dropped their code. Today, a typical "one-hour" prime-time show has about forty-two minutes of content and eighteen minutes of ads and promotions, nearly twice the advertising intensity of two decades ago.

What if we managed advertising as we manage, or could manage, physical pollution? If corporations want to pollute our minds, they'd have to pay for the right to do so. As with physical pollution, the transactions could be brokered by a trust. This guardian of our inner commons would set caps on total trespasses and sell tradeable advertising permits to corporations. Our psychic costs would then show up as advertisers' monetary costs. There'd be less advertising, more peace of mind, and if we so earmarked the revenue, more money for commercial-free broadcasting and the arts.

An advertising cap-and-trade system could have another benefit as well. At present, there's only one macroeconomic valve for regulating the pace of economic activity: the Fed's handle on money. If the economy is too hot, the Fed raises interest rates; if it's too cool, the Fed lowers them. The trouble with this valve is that it has unpleasant side effects. When interest rates go up, so do credit card bills and mortgages, and millions of households suffer. But if we dampened an overheated economy by lowering the volume of advertising, we'd get the benefits of higher interest rates without the pain. In fact, households might *save* money by buying less.

The Airwaves

The airwaves, also known as the broadcast spectrum, are a gift of nature that modern technology has turned into a valuable resource. As a medium for sharing information and ideas, airwaves have enormous advantages over paper and wires. The problem in the early days was that signals often interfered with one another. If two nearby transmitters used the same or adjacent frequencies, a radio listener would hear two sound streams simultaneously. America's approach to this problem (though not Britain's or Canada's) was to give free exclusive local frequencies to private broadcasters, subject to periodic hearings and renewal.

The quid pro quo for this gift, according to the Communications Act of 1934, was that broadcasters would serve "the public interest, convenience, and necessity"—whatever that might mean. The airwaves themselves would remain, in theory, public property, with the Federal Communications Commission (again in theory) acting as trustee.

Private broadcasters grew large and profitable under this arrangement. But over time, as their advertising revenues soared, their public-interest obligations declined. In the 1980s, the FCC dropped the Fairness Doctrine, which required broadcasters to air both sides of controversial issues. Educational programming also waned.

In the 1990s the spread of cell phones created huge new demand for airwaves. Instead of giving frequencies to cell phone companies for free, Congress wisely chose to auction them, raising billions of dollars for the federal treasury. Broadcasters, however, lobbied hard for more free spectrum, and in 1996 Congress gave it to them, ostensibly for digital TV. This was the $70 billion giveaway I described earlier.

Today, digital technology makes it possible for "smart" receivers to pick out only the signals they need. Signal interference thus is, or soon could be, a thing of the past—which makes exclusive licenses unnecessary. The airwaves could be an open access commons with virtually no capacity limits, a possibility that makes broadcasters, phone, and cable companies extremely anxious.

Some broadcasters have another idea. They want to privatize the airwaves, with ownership assigned to them. Under this plan, the free licenses they received for digital TV would become permanent entitlements usable for any purpose. Broadcasters could then sell their entitlements to cell phone companies and pocket the windfall. The big winners would be General Electric (NBC), Disney (ABC), and Rupert Murdoch (Fox). Other beneficiaries would include Pat Robertson (Christian Broadcasting Network) and Lowell "Bud" Paxson (Pax TV). When a reporter asked Paxson why he should receive millions of dollars for selling the public's airwaves, he replied: "I was a farmer and I got lucky. Now people want to build a mall on my farm. God bless America."

If Congress treated the airwaves as a common asset, it would lease most of them at market rates for limited terms to the highest bidders. The billions of dollars thus raised could buy free airtime for political candidates, fund noncommercial radio and TV, and help sustain the arts.

Alternatively, Congress could turn the airwaves into an open access commons like roads and streets. Using technologies like wi-fi (wireless fidelity), everyone could enjoy high-speed Internet access for almost nothing. As of early 2006, nearly 150 U.S. cities were deploying or planning public wi-fi networks. These efforts are hampered by the fact that the frequencies allotted to wi-fi don't travel as far, or penetrate buildings as well, as do the frequencies given to broadcasters. A bill to open unused TV channels for wi-fi has been introduced by a group of senators, but it faces stiff opposition from broadcasters, telephone, and cable companies.

The Internet

The Internet is a human-made commons that, for all intents and purposes, can be used without limit. It's arguably the most remarkable technological achievement of the twentieth century, given that it revolutionizes commerce, community, and culture in one swoop. As with other valuable commons, it's coveted by private corporations. The battle in coming years will be between those who want to privatize big chunks of the Internet, and those (including many corporations) who want it to be as free, universal, and open as possible. What's unusual is that this is one of the few battlegrounds where those on the side of the commons have an early edge.

One looming battle concerns access—in particular, bridging the "last mile" between the Internet and the millions of people (billions worldwide) who *could* use it, but now don't. When the Internet began, the last mile was typically crossed by telephone. A user would dial up an Internet server and log on. However, because telephone wires were sized for voice signals, they can't carry high volumes of data at high speeds.

In due time, cable companies began offering their thicker cables to Internet users. Phone companies also came up with a system— DSL—that squeezes more data through their skinny wires. There are thus now two good ways to get high-speed access to the Internet—*if* you can afford roughly $30 a month, or $360 a year. Since not everyone can afford this, however, we have what some people call a *digital divide*—a financial barrier to universal access.

This is where the airwaves come in. Using digital signals, it's now possible to bridge the last mile to the Internet through the public's own airwaves. Not only that, it's incredibly cheap to do so, using technologies like wi-fi. At the same time, another technical breakthrough is imminent: the Internet—including this last wireless mile—will soon be "thick" enough to carry data, telephone calls, and television pictures. In theory, a small public investment could bring all these services to the doorsteps of virtually everyone. There'd be no more need for private TV networks, telephone and cable companies. The so-called information highway would be, like public streets, truly open and free.

This is an extraordinary possibility. Americans now pay some $300 billion a year for telephone and cable services; perhaps half of this could be saved. That's the equivalent of raising every worker's take-home pay by about $1,000 a year. It should be cause for celebration.

What's more, free universal Internet access would be a boon to the corporate side of the economy—another example of a commons having positive external benefits. Think of an urban shopping street, or Main Street in a small town. Merchants on these streets depend on foot traffic; the more passersby, the more sales they make. If someone put checkpoints or tollbooths on these streets, merchants would scream. So it is with the Internet. Everyone doing business on the Internet wants more traffic. Making the Internet free to all would be the best thing that ever happened to merchants.

Except, of course, for the phone-and-cable duopoly. In several states, these powerful companies have pushed through laws prohibiting cities from offering wireless Internet service, and they've sponsored a similar ban in Congress. The companies say their right to profit trumps the consumer's right to save money and a city's right to serve its citizens. Many politicians still buy that argument, so the end of this story has yet to be written.

A similar battle looms over what's called "net neutrality." At the moment, the Internet—like the telephone system—treats all content equally. No one's data is discriminated against, and no one's gets favored either—your personal webste is treated the same as Google's. However, cable and phone companies want to create a two-tiered Internet, with some content providers getting slow speed and others—who pay the phone and cable companies—getting high speed. That would mean more revenue for the companies, but also a permanent divide between corporate content providers and everyone else. Congress is now considering bills both to allow and to ban such tiering, and the outcome as this is written is uncertain.

Patently Unscientific

Enclosure of the commons has also been occurring in the world of science. Here, too, the Founders' intentions were clear. Ben Franklin, no slouch when it came to the dollar, never sought a patent on his most famous invention, the Franklin stove. "As we enjoy great advantages from the inventions of others," he wrote, "we should be glad to serve others by any invention of ours." Thomas Jefferson, who served as first head of the U.S. Patent Office, believed the purpose of the office was to *promulgate* inventions, not protect them. He rejected nearly half the applications submitted during his term. (Eli Whitney's cotton gin made it through.)

As with copyrights, this stringent approach to patents worked well for a long time. America didn't lack inventiveness in the nineteenth and early twentieth centuries (and let it be remembered that we stole much of our early technology from the British). But from midcentury to the present, patenting has become a national pastime. The Bayh-Dole Act of 1980, which let universities get patents on taxpayer-funded research and license those patents to corporations, opened the floodgates. Corporate money rushed into academic labs, and with it came a corporate mindset. Where scientists once shared their discoveries openly, many now fear to discuss them, lest someone beat them to the patent office. Today, some say, the secrecy is so intense and the thicket of property rights so dense that the advancement of research has noticeably slowed.

The U.S. Patent Office has gone along with this, issuing patents for everything from one-click shopping on the Internet to genes that are 99 percent nature-made. Often, companies get patents not with the intention of developing them, but rather with the intention of suing someone else who might (a practice known as *patent trolling*). Figure 8.1 shows the dramatic rise in number of patents issued over the past few decades.

Consumers and taxpayers are burdened as well. Thanks to patents, pharmaceutical companies can charge monopoly prices for up to twenty years after introducing a new drug. This is said to benefit society by providing incentives for research, but according to the Center for Economic Policy Research, the benefit is greatly exceeded by the cost. Pharmaceutical companies spend about $25 billion a year on research, of which about 70 percent is for copycat drugs that mimic competitors' brands and add no significant health benefits.

Figure 8.1
U.S. PATENTS ISSUED, 1860–2005

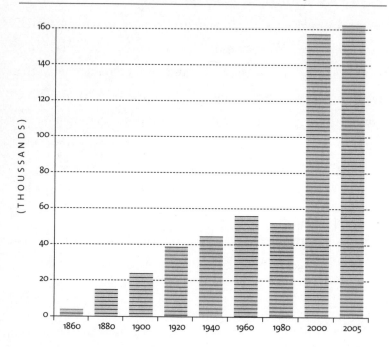

Source: U.S. Patent and Trademark Office.

The federal government could fund 100 percent of noncopycat research—and place the resulting drugs in the public domain—entirely from cost savings to Medicare and Medicaid. On top of that, the savings to consumers from lower drug costs would amount to hundreds of billions of dollars each year.

To release science from corporate control, we need to take a twofold approach: apply more stringent standards for issuing patents, and provide more public funds for research (with the proviso that publicly funded discoveries stay in the public domain). The track record for publicly funded research has, in fact, been phenomenal. The entire computer industry was spawned by the U.S. Army Ordnance Corps, which produced the first digital computer in 1945. Similarly, the Internet emerged from the Defense Advanced Research Projects Agency and the National Science Foundation in the 1980s. It's hard to imagine the modern world without either of these breakthroughs, or with the Internet being owned, say, by Verizon or TimeWarner.

Fortify, Then Enhance

The larger lesson of this chapter is that all three branches of the commons—nature, community, and culture—are under similar assault from corporations, and all need to be fortified. The means of fortification will vary with the particular commons. When commons are scarce or threatened, we ought to limit aggregate use, assign property rights to trusts, and charge market prices to users. When commons are limitless (like culture, the Internet, and potentially the airwaves), our challenge is the opposite: to provide the greatest benefit to the greatest number at the lowest cost. To create scarcity where it doesn't need to exist diminishes rather than enlarges our well-being.

In both limited and unlimited commons, corporate and commons algorithms clash. In limited commons, the corporate algorithm says: use as much as you can as quickly as you can, because if you don't, someone else will. The commons algorithm, by contrast, says: preserve the asset for future generations, enhance it whenever possible, and live off income rather than principal. In unlimited commons, the corporate algorithm says: restrict use and charge what the market will bear. The commons algorithm, by contrast, says: the more users the merrier, and the cheaper the better. In both situations, the commons algorithm conflicts head-on with the corporate one, and that's just fine. Indeed, it's precisely the point.

Commons algorithms need to be unleashed in real-time markets, where they can duke it out with their corporate counterparts. Managers in each sector will know what to do, and the public will know what to expect. If corporations keep winning, then add more property to the commons. Eventually, we'll get the best of both worlds, and when there's conflict, more balanced outcomes than we get today. We'll also gain clarity about the real costs of current practices.

After we fortify, we should enhance; just as we take from the commons, so should we give back. Art and music can be reproduced by corporations, but they don't *come* from corporations; they come from the commons. Folk music, country music, jazz, blues, garage bands—these are the roots of our musical heritage. We must nourish the soil in which these roots grow. This, not copyright extension, is the way to enrich culture.

Part 3

MAKING IT
HAPPEN

Chapter 9

Building the Commons Sector

If you don't know where you're going,
you probably won't get there.
—*Yogi Berra*

M y sons play a computer game called *Sim City.* It's a brilliant
invention that lets you design, grow, and govern your own virtual metropolis. You plunk down streets, sewers, power systems, and
subways. You zone for commerce, industry, and residences. You drop
in schools, hospitals, and fire stations. Soon a city comes to life. It's
enough to engross kids for hours.

Now imagine an adult game called *Sim Commons* that lets you
design and grow your own virtual economic sector. The object of the
game is to produce the most happiness with the least destruction of
nature. You plunk down commons trusts, and from simple menus
you assign them property rights, ownership regimes, and management algorithms. As you play, the computer displays your happiness
and nature scores. Through trial and error, you learn what combina-
tions of moves work best.

In the real world, building a new commons sector will be
something like that. While we wait for an historic shift at the

national level, we can build and experiment at lower levels. We can test different kinds of trusts, nonprofits, and informal associations, seeing how closely they can hew to commons principles. Then, when history is ready for bigger changes, we'll be ready too.

In this chapter I'll describe some of the models we'll want to replicate and refine. I'll start locally and move upward, saving global thoughts for the chapter's conclusion. My aim is twofold: first, to celebrate seeds that are already emerging, and second, to suggest how, taken together and multiplied, these seeds can grow into a sector powerful enough to balance the corporate sector. Figure 9.1 gives an idea of what the commons sector will look like at the local, regional, and national levels.

Local Initiatives

"Where's the action?" the gamblers ask in *Guys and Dolls*. When it comes to building local commons institutions, the action is just about everywhere. Here's a sampler.

LAND TRUSTS

I've already mentioned the Marin Agricultural Land Trust and the Pacific Forest Trust. The aim of such trusts is to shield pieces of land from development or degradation. They do this by owning land outright, or by owning easements that restrict how land may be used.

Land trusts aren't just for the countryside. In Boston, people in the Dudley Street neighborhood formed one in 1988 to buy vacant land and determine how it could best serve the community. Today there are six hundred new and rehabbed homes—all with a cap on resale prices—plus gardens, a common area, parks, and playgrounds. These efforts revitalized the neighborhood without displacing local residents, as would have happened through private property and gentrification.

Figure 9.1
THE NEW COMMONS SECTOR

National
- American Permanent Fund
- Children's start-up trust
- Universal health insurance
- Copyright royalty fund
- Spectrum trust
- Commons tax credit...

Regional
- Regional watershed trusts
- Regional airshed trusts
- Mississippi basin trust
- Buffalo comons...

Local
- Land trusts
- Municipal wi-fi
- Community gardens
- Farmers' markets
- Public spaces
- Car-free zones
- Time banks...

Managed Global Commons

Open Cultural Commons

SURFACE WATER TRUSTS

The Oregon Water Trust, founded in 1993, acquires surface water rights to protect salmon and other fish. So far it has worked with over three hundred landowners to put water back into streams, some of which had been sucked completely dry. Sometimes a water rights seller forgoes water by switching crops, or by irrigating only during the spring, when stream flows are ample for farmers and fish alike. At other times, deals have hinged on delivering water from a different source, while leaving it in streams where fish need it. Recently, similar trusts have sprung up in Montana, Colorado, New Mexico, Texas, Washington, and Nevada.

GROUNDWATER TRUSTS

Groundwater, the source of half of America's drinking water, is being pumped faster than nature replenishes it. The problem is especially acute in the High Plains, where farmers are depleting the Ogallala Aquifer, and in the Southwest, where many cities face water shortages. In San Antonio, which gets 99 percent of its water from the Edwards Aquifer, the Edwards Aquifer Authority now limits groundwater withdrawals by issuing permits. A similar trust for the Ogallala Aquifer is a solution waiting to happen.

COMMUNITY GARDENS

Turn the corner in Manhattan and you may discover a green oasis rising from the rubble of a vacant lot. Amid the bean vines and tomato plants stand sculptures, shrines, and toolsheds, all on land the gardeners claimed after buildings had been demolished. New York City is dotted with 700 community gardens. About 150 of these will eventually give way to housing, but the rest will stay.

And it's not just New York. The American Community Gardening Association counts seventy major cities with community gardens. In Seattle, more than nineteen hundred families raise food in these neighborhood spaces. In Philadelphia, gardeners save an estimated $700 each year on food bills. In Boston, the Food Project produces over 120,000 pounds of vegetables on twenty-one acres; most of it goes to people in need. Just as importantly, these gardens turn strangers into neighbors.

FARMERS' MARKETS

Until the Civil War, most American cities had public food markets. In the 1940s, there was a brief resurgence, as farmers sought better prices and shoppers sought fresher food. Then came interstate highways, and the market for seasonal local produce collapsed.

Now these commercial commons are being reestablished. From Union Square in New York City to San Francisco's Ferry Building, city-dwellers are rediscovering the pleasures of meeting each other and the people who produce their food. There are now nearly four thousand farmers' markets in the fifty states, double the number that existed ten years ago.

PUBLIC SPACES

From New York City's Bryant Park to Portland, Oregon's, Pioneer Square to Boston's Copley Square, urban plazas are coming back to life. Even Detroit, which was built by the automobile, is reviving its downtown by rerouting autos around a new public square called Campus Martius Park. The park bristles with life in both summer and winter, and has attracted some $500 million in new investment to the area.

In Portland, informal groups of neighbors have reclaimed street intersections. They paint vivid designs on the pavement to mark the place as their own, and often add community-building amenities such as produce stands and play areas.

TIME BANKS

Helping your neighbor is an American tradition. But as people relocate more frequently, it's harder for them to trust that favors they do will be repaid. Time banks are one solution.

The idea is simplicity itself. When you help a neighbor for an hour, you earn one "time dollar." Then, when you need help, you can spend your saved dollars. In Brooklyn, New York, members of an HMO for the elderly use such temporal currency to help each other with home repairs, transportation, and companionship. It's a model waiting to be replicated.

MUNICIPAL WI-FI

The Internet is the sidewalk of the twenty-first century, so it's not surprising that cities are starting to build high-speed wireless networks the way they once built streets. Many operate wireless "hot zones" that offer free access over dozens of blocks. In San Francisco and New Orleans, free access may even be citywide. Other cities, like Philadelphia, are rolling out low-cost service citywide.

Regional Initiatives

Some commons are regional in scale and require regional management. The examples that follow are in the early stages of conception, design, and implementation.

AIR TRUSTS

While the federal government dallies on climate change, several states are taking action. Most advanced is the Regional Greenhouse Gas Initiative, launched by seven northeastern states from Maine to Delaware. Their plan will limit carbon dioxide emissions from power plants and require utilities to hold emission permits. Still undecided as of mid-2006 is a crucial question: will polluters pay for their permits, or will they get most of them for free?

Dozens of citizens' groups are calling upon the states to auction emission permits and use the proceeds to reduce costs to consumers. "Historically, polluters have used our air for free," says Marc Breslow of the Massachusetts Climate Action Network. "But there's no justification for allowing them to keep doing so. The atmosphere is common property."

As this is written, some politicians are listening. The Vermont legislature voted to auction 100 percent of the state's emission permits, rather than give them free to polluters. In Massachusetts, a key committee approved a five-year transition to full auctioning—though the state's governor, Mitt Romney, abruptly withdrew Massachusetts from the regional initiative. In New York, the state attorney general, Eliot Spitzer, announced his support for 100 percent auctioning. This could be especially significant if Spitzer, as seems likely, becomes governor in 2007.

WATERSHED TRUSTS

In the 1930s, there was the Tennessee Valley Authority. Its main job was to control floods and bring electricity to a seven-state region. Today a watershed trust's missions would be different: to protect rivers and fish, and to promote sustainable agriculture.

Consider our largest watershed, the Missouri-Mississippi-Ohio, which drains water and waste from twenty-five states into the Gulf of Mexico. In the mid-1980s, fishers in the Gulf noticed a growing "dead zone" during summer months, when fish and crustacean populations plummeted. According to the EPA, the dead zone has now swelled to some five thousand square miles. The problem is *hypoxia,* or absence of dissolved oxygen. The proximate cause is overabundant algae growth that triggers a cascade of effects that ultimately sucks oxygen out of the water.

What causes aquatic plants to grow so fast they overwhelm an entire ecosystem? In a word, nutrients—the same nutrients (nitrogen and phosphorous) that farmers feed to their terrestrial crops. Excess nutrients run off the soil and are washed down the Mississippi. In 1997, an interagency task force was created to study the problem and recommend solutions. In 2001 it called for "voluntary, practical, and cost-effective" actions by industry and government. Unfortunately, so far not much has happened.

What if we considered the topsoil and flowing waters of the Mississippi basin as a commons to be preserved for future generations? We might, then, create a Mississippi Soil and Water Trust.

The trust would hold all rights to introduce fertilizers (and perhaps pesticides and herbicides) within the basin. Its job would be to reduce chemical inputs to safe levels and to reward farmers (and others) for proper stewardship of their land.

Each year the trust would sell a declining number of tradeable soil input permits; manufacturers would bid for these. It would then recycle revenue from permit sales to landowners who meet steward-ship guidelines. This would raise the cost of chemical-intensive agri-culture while rewarding farmers for being good land stewards. Farmers' crop yields might decline for a while, but their incomes wouldn't. In a decade or two, the Gulf would come back to life, and farming in America's heartland would be a lot more organic. The transition time would depend on the rate at which the trust decreases the number of permits it issues.

BUFFALO COMMONS

The Great Plains have been called America's lost Serengeti. Once, mil-lions of bison, antelope, and elk roamed here, sustainably hunted by native tribes. When European settlers arrived, so did cattle, wheat, and fences. Soon the big wild animals were all but exterminated.

The Great Plains boomed for a while, but declined after the 1920s. By the 1980s, population had plunged, soil erosion was at Dust Bowl levels, and the Ogallala Aquifer, the source of much of the region's water, was dropping fast. In 1987, geographers Deborah and Frank Popper proposed a long-term restoration concept they called the *Buffalo Commons*.

The metaphor sparked the region's imagination. Meetings were held, studies conducted, task forces formed. What emerged is a move-ment to reestablish a corridor large enough for bison and other native wildlife to roam freely. This unfenced prairie, perhaps ten or twenty million acres in size, would not only restore some of the bison's lost habitat; it would turn the whole region into a high-quality place to live. The Nature Conservancy and similar entities are now trying to build this commons piece by piece.

National Initiatives

Commons organizing principles are scalable; the same rules that work locally and regionally can also be applied nationally. Generally, it's best to organize commons at the lowest level possible; that increases community involvement and transparency. Sometimes, though, the scale of the underlying commons is so large that the management structure must be national or international. Here are examples of possible national institutions.

AN AMERICAN PERMANENT FUND

An American Permanent Fund would be the centerpiece of the new commons sector proposed in this volume. It's a way to fix, or at least ameliorate, capitalism's flaw of concentrating private property among the top 5 percent of the population. It would do this, like the Alaska Permanent Fund, by distributing income from common property to every citizen equally. This would add a third set of "pipes" through which income would flow to Americans, the first two being wages and private property income.

As discussed in chapter 7, the American Permanent Fund's income would come in part from the sale of pollution permits—mostly for carbon dioxide—and in part from the commons' share of corporate profits. The first revenue source would be directly correlated to our efforts to curb global warming. If we decided to reduce carbon dioxide emissions, say, by 3 percent per year for the next three decades, as scientists say we must, this would generate a substantial flow of income into the American Permanent Fund. Some of that might be invested or spent on public goods, and some would be used for per capita dividends. The faster we reduced emissions, the higher these dividends would be. In effect, the dividends and public goods would be a bonus to Americans for doing the right ecological thing.

Eventually, when a post-carbon infrastructure is built, carbon emissions would stabilize at a low level, and so would this revenue source for the American Permanent Fund. By this time, the second revenue source—dividends from holding a portion of publicly traded corporate shares—would kick in. This revenue source would give every citizen a stake in increasing corporate profits, just as the first source gives them a stake in decreasing pollution. Who could object to that combination?

Getting the Permanent Fund up and running, even if it starts small, would be a crucial precedent and signal. Like the Social Security Trust Fund, it would be a pipeline through which more money would flow over time. It would establish a fundamental principle for the commons sector—one person, one share. And it would change the way Americans think about our economic relationship with nature: every penny *not* paid by a polluter would be a penny out of everyone's pocket. It wouldn't be just future generations, then, who experience a loss when nature is degraded; the bank accounts of living Americans would suffer as well. Irresponsibility toward the future would carry an immediate and widely felt price.

THE CHILDREN'S OPPORTUNITY TRUST

The Children's Opportunity Trust is the second big piece of national commons infrastructure. It's a way to fix capitalism's other bad habit of perpetuating class privileges from one generation to the next.

Unlike feudalism, which was based on hereditary aristocracy, capitalism is, in theory, a meritocracy, or at least a "luckocracy." Players are supposed to have a fair, if not equal, chance to succeed.

Winners are supposed to be determined by hard work, talent, and luck, rather than by accident of birth. Yet, as we've seen, Capitalism 2.0 falls far short of this ideal.

The Children's Opportunity Trust would give every child, as a birthright, an infusion of start-up capital—a kind of Social Security for the front end of life. The trust's revenue would come from end-of-life repayments, as explained in chapter 7. This funding mechanism, I believe, is better than taking money from the general treasury. It directly links start-up help from society with an end-of-life obligation to repay, creating a kind of temporal commons that connects arriving and departing generations.

A SPECTRUM TRUST

A spectrum or airwaves trust would have a distinct mission: to reduce the influence of corporations on our democracy. Its economic and ecological impacts could be significant (reducing corporate political influence will improve many policies), but they're secondary to the political objective.

According to a study by the New America Foundation, the market value of the airwave licenses we've given free to corporate broadcasters is roughly $500 billion. It's possible this value will decline as unlicensed wi-fi spreads, but meanwhile broadcasters sell our airwaves to advertisers and reap billions that belong, at least in part, to all of us.

Part of that money comes from political candidates who must purchase TV and radio ads to get elected. The problem isn't so much the unearned windfall broadcasters collect; rather, it's the fact that candidates are compelled to pay it to them. That makes politicians kowtow to corporate donors in order to pay broadcasters. Other democracies give free airtime to political candidates, but we protect the broadcasters' lock on our airwaves. By privatizing our airwaves, in other words, we've effectively privatized our democracy. The job of a spectrum trust would be to take back our democracy by taking back our airwaves.

This could be done in a couple of ways. One wouldn't require an actual trust: Congress could simply say that, in exchange for free spectrum licenses, broadcasters must give a certain amount of free airtime to political candidates. Alternatively, broadcasters could pay for their licenses, with revenue going to a nonpartisan trust. That trust would allocate funds to candidates for the purchase of TV and radio ads; the allocation formula would take account of cost differences between media markets and other relevant variables. Neither of these approaches would prevent corporations from lobbying or contributing to candidates' other expenses, but they *would* level the political playing field by greatly reducing the sums candidates have to raise to get elected.

COMMONS TAX CREDITS

Some commons trusts will generate income from the sale of usage permits. Many others will *need* income to acquire property rights, restore degraded habitat, or give children start-up capital. It's therefore essential to encourage a multiplicity of revenue sources. The best way to do this is through a federal commons tax credit.

When I was in the solar energy business during the 1970s, our customers benefited from a combination of federal and state solar tax credits. As I frequently explained then, a tax credit isn't the same as a tax deduction—it's bigger. A deduction is subtracted from the amount of income subject to tax; if your marginal tax rate is 30 percent, a tax *deduction* saves you thirty cents on the dollar. By contrast, a tax *credit* is subtracted from the amount of taxes you pay, regardless of your tax bracket. If you owe taxes, it always saves you one hundred cents on the dollar.

The premise behind a commons tax credit is that wealthy Americans owe more to the commons than they currently pay to the government in taxes. That being so, a commons tax credit would work like this. The federal government would raise the uppermost tax bracket by a few percentage points. At the same time, it would give affected taxpayers a choice: pay the extra money to the government, or contribute it to one or more qualified commons trusts. If people do the latter, they get a 100 percent tax credit, thereby avoiding additional taxes. The message to the wealthy thus is: *You have to give back more. Whether you give it to the IRS or directly to the commons is up to you. If you want to eliminate the government middleman, that's fine.*

What qualifies as a commons trust? It's a trust that either benefits all citizens more or less equally or collects money to restore an endangered commons. Social Security, the American Permanent Fund, the Children's Opportunity Trust, and most land and watershed trusts, would qualify. By contrast, a normal charity would not. Contributions to normal charities would remain deductible from taxable income, but not from taxes owed.

Global Initiatives

According to a near-unanimous consensus of scientists, the world is very close to a tipping point on atmospheric carbon: we must drastically curtail our carbon burning or climate hell will soon break loose. This means every nation must install economy-wide valves for reducing their carbon use. I described earlier how America might do this using a carbon, or sky trust. Since we can't halt global warming by ourselves, however, the necessary complement to such an American trust is a global trust.

A global carbon trust would require national governments to recognize that, just as they can, and should, delegate *internal* trustee-ship duties to trusts, so should they delegate *global* trusteeship duties. The alternative, I'd argue, is paralysis in the face of clear and present danger.

Consider the long and tortuous climate negotiations that began in the early 1990s. They produced, first, a toothless pledge by all nations—the Rio Convention of 1992—to voluntarily reduce their greenhouse gas emissions to the 1990 level by 2010. Five years later, they produced a slightly toothier protocol in Kyoto, which took another five years to ratify and translate into operational rules. An equally prolonged negotiation now looms for the successor to Kyoto, which expires in 2012.

No doubt these negotiations could move faster if the current U.S. administration weren't so obstinately opposed to them. But the deeper problem is that nearly two hundred sovereign nations are trying to negotiate a deal that satisfies everyone. The process is inherently cumbersome, and not surprisingly, the results fall far short of what scientists say is necessary. Perhaps, therefore, it's time to delegate.

I can imagine a global atmosphere trust working something like this. It would be governed by a smallish board of trustees and a general membership consisting of all signatory nations. The general membership would appoint the trustees. There might be, as in the U.N. Security Council, a number of seats reserved for "great powers" (in this case, large emitters) and another number set aside for regions. However, once trustees are appointed, their loyalty would shift from individual nations or regions to future generations. This is critical.

The trustees would decide, based on peer-reviewed scientific evidence, where to set a global cap on carbon emissions. Each year, they'd issue tradeable carbon emission permits up to that year's limit. A portion of these permits (initially, a majority) would be distributed at no cost to participating nations based on a pre-agreed formula. The remainder would be auctioned by the trust, with the revenue used to remediate damage caused by climate change and aid the inevitable victims. The trust would determine on a yearly basis how many permits were needed for these purposes, and how the remediation funds would be spent.

The trustees would make decisions by majority vote, with no vetoes. Like a court, they'd explain their decisions in writing, showing exactly how they protect future generations. The general membership could override a trustee decision by, say, a two-thirds majority. In this way, signatory nations *could* put short-term interests over long-term ones, but they'd have to do so explicitly, and implicitly admit to stealing or borrowing from future generations.

The knotty question is, What formula should be used to distribute carbon emission permits among nations? The key to crafting such a formula, given the disparate interests of so many nations, is to ground it on some universal principle of equity. The Kyoto Protocol didn't do this; it was a hodgepodge of deals and escape hatches aimed at pleasing the United States, which in the end didn't ratify anyway. The next international regime, however, must appeal to the poor and the up-and-coming, as well as to the United States and other developed countries. Without an organizing principle based on equity, it's hard to see how any deal can be reached.

Fortunately, an equitable organizing principle has been advanced: it's known as *contract and converge*. Here's how it would work.

First, an overall reduction schedule would be agreed to; this is the *contract* part of the equation. Then, rights to the global

atmospheric commons would be divided among nations in proportion to their populations—in other words, one person, one share.
However, absolute proportionality wouldn't kick in for a decade or
two, during which time the allocation formula would *converge* toward
proportionality. The *rate* of convergence would be a topic for
negotiation; the *goal* of per capita equity would be accepted at
the outset.

Before and after convergence, poor and populous countries with
more permits than emissions could sell their excess permits to rich
and relatively underpopulated countries that are short on them. In
this way, nations could pollute at different levels, with overusers of
the atmosphere paying underusers for the privilege. Americans could,
in other words, extend our present level of carbon use for another
decade or so, but we'd have to pay poor countries to do so.

Would a global atmospheric trust be too great a surrender of
national sovereignty? I think not. We're not talking about world government here. We're talking about a trust to manage a specific worldwide commons. The one and only job of that trust would be to set
and enforce limits on certain emissions into that commons. Some loss
of sovereignty is involved, but less than we've already yielded to the
World Trade Organization. Compared to the benefit we and all
nations would gain—a stabilized climate—our loss of sovereignty
would be small potatoes.

If a global atmosphere trust could be established, it would be a
watershed twenty-first-century event. Geopolitically, it could lay the
foundation for a harmonious century, much as the Versailles Treaty
paved the way for a disharmonious one in the twentieth. It would
also help the world deal gracefully with the decline in global oil
production that experts say is imminent.

Economically, a global atmosphere trust would spur some important changes. Corporations the world over would immediately pour money into energy efficiency and noncarbon energy infrastructure. There'd be a rush to deploy new technologies. Economies—including ours—would boom, not *despite* higher carbon prices, but *because* of them.

Why would this happen? The simplest reason is that a global atmosphere trust would remove an enormous cloud of uncertainty. Businesses would see the future of carbon burning, and be more confident that a price shock—more damaging than a gradual rise—wouldn't derail their plans. Such a trust would also remove a major source of international tension—the scramble for declining oil supplies—that could easily lead to war. In addition, the flow of money to poor countries (from sales of emission permits to rich countries) would lift their economies and wages, help U.S. exports and slow U.S. job loss. All these things would ensure that while high-carbon activity declines, low-carbon activity rises at a comparable rate.

But growth in aggregate economic activity isn't the only benefit we'd see; qualitative improvements would also occur. Thus, as long-distance transport costs rose, manufacturers would shift from global to local production. Farmers would return to practices they used before cheap petrochemicals became available. They'd grow more food organically and sell more through farmers' markets and urban buying clubs, cutting out middlemen and keeping more of their products' value. For nonperishables, consumers would shop more on the Internet and less at drive-and-haul malls. Thanks to eBay, Craigslist, and similar services, they'd also buy more secondhand goods and dump fewer into landfills. More workers would ride bikes, jitneys, and trains, and work online from home. Cities would favor footpower, suburbs would reorganize around transit hubs, and new forms of co-housing would spread. All these changes would be profitable and even exciting. And they'd proceed with relative smoothness if we placed the global atmosphere in trust.

On the other hand, if we leave our atmosphere as an unmanaged waste dump, our glorious industrial party will abruptly end, brought to its knees by oil price shocks, climate disasters, or a monetary panic. After that, no one can know what will happen. That's the stark choice we face.

The Role of Government

One of the most valuable lessons I learned in business was, when you need something done, find the right person, give that person clear marching orders, authority, and resources, and get out of the way. In other words, delegate.

The same logic applies to government. When government wants to do things, it has to find people to do them. It can add people to its own bureaucracy, or it can contract with outsiders. It shouldn't matter as long as the public purpose is met at reasonable cost.

When it comes to building the new commons sector, there's plenty for everyone to do. Government in particular has four important roles to play:

1. Until it assigns responsibility for a commons to someone else, government is the default trustee, and should be held to trusteeship standards.
2. Government is the initial assigner and ultimate arbiter of property rights. Instead of privatizing nearly everything, it should assign more property rights to commons trusts and give commons rights precedence over capital's.

3. Only government can broker inter- and intragenerational compacts like Social Security and Medicare. We need government to do this again for health insurance and the Children's Opportunity Trust.

4. Government can help finance the reacquisition and restoration of previously privatized pieces of the commons. State and local governments in particular have the authority to issue long-term tax-exempt bonds, which can be used to acquire private land and water rights.

These four roles reflect government's unique responsibilities and strengths. But there are areas where government *doesn't* have a competitive advantage, and much of this book has been about one of them.

Earlier I discussed the trusteeship function—the work that *someone* must do to protect our shared inheritances. We need this function to work right, because if it doesn't, our descendants, along with many other species' offspring, are doomed. So we have to ask, who is best suited to perform this function? The evidence suggests that neither government nor private corporations can do this particular job well. So we're left with trusts that are accountable to future generations.

I suggest to those who care about the future: *it's time to delegate the trusteeship function to trusts.* We should give the trusts clear missions, authority, and resources, and then get out of their way. The trusts may not be perfect, but they're likely to do a better job, for a longer time, than any of the known alternatives.

Chapter 10

What You Can Do

Two roads diverged in a wood, and I—
I took the one less traveled by,
And that has made all the difference.
—Robert Frost, 1920

We come at last to the inescapable question: What can each of us do to help build Capitalism 3.0?

Earlier, I noted that corporations dominate American government most, but not all, of the time. Once or twice per century, there are brief openings during which noncorporate forces reign. No one can say *when* the next such opening will occur, but it's safe to say that it *will*. We must be ready when it comes to build a strong, self-perpetuating commons sector, not easily dismantled when the political wheel turns again.

Being ready *then* means getting busy *now*. We should, first of all, start noticing and talking about our common wealth. Whenever we see it, we should point to it and let the world know to whom it belongs.

Second, we should demand more birthrights and property rights than we have now. Rights that belong to everyone. Rights built into our operating system. Rights that protect future generations as well as our own.

The reason I stress property rights is that, in America, property rights are sacred. They're guaranteed by the Constitution. Once you have them, they can't be taken without fair compensation. These protections have greatly benefited those who own private property. They should also benefit those who share common wealth.

Third, we should imagine and design multiple pieces of the commons sector—that is, *organized forms* we want the commons to take. And we should build and test our models wherever possible. Frequently in the past, models developed locally have both replicated on their own, and risen to the national level. That's how Social Security and many of our environmental laws emerged.

Roles for All

To build Capitalism 3.0, we each have unique roles to play. I therefore address the final pages of this book to a variety of people whose participation is critical.

PARENTS

You want the best for your children. You want them to be safe, to fulfill their potential, to pursue happiness. What, then, will you leave to them? I'm not talking about money; I'm talking about nonfinancial gifts—a strong community, a vibrant culture, a healthy planet. Can you—can we—leave those kinds of gifts?

Yes, we can—*if* we join with others. And there are many ways to join. We can do it face-to-face, or online with like-minded strangers. We can do it through organizations and elections. We can do it in our churches, synagogues, and mosques.

No one can single-handedly change a community, or America, or the world. But we *can* join with others to do so. Who, how, and what you join is entirely up to you. That you do it, and do it this year, is my request.

WAGE EARNERS

You had it good for a while. Thanks to labor unions, you lifted your-selves into the middle class. You got paid vacations, forty-hour work-weeks, time-and-half for overtime, health insurance, a pension, and most of all, job security. Even companies without unions paid well and offered lifetime employment if you wanted it. There was a social contract, if not a legal one, between employers, workers, and commu-nities. This was America's version of the welfare state, and if you were part of it, it wasn't bad. But those days are dust.

In today's global marketplace, capital moves at the speed of light, and you're just a cost to be minimized. What management seeks—what capital *demands*—is more profit next quarter. Did you give the best years of your life to Acme Inc.? Too bad. Nothing boosts the bottom line faster than downsizing, outsourcing, or playing games with your pension fund. And forget about help from the union; it's toothless now. We're all on our own.

What can you do? Truthfully, not much. In the era of global capital, your form of income—wages—is at a serious competitive disadvantage. But over time, things can get better. The way out—for your kids, if not for you—is through a new version of capitalism that gives you (and everyone else) *property income* from a share of common wealth. That share is your birthright. It can't be downsized or out-sourced. It pays some dividends in cash, and others in no-fuss health care, free Internet access, healthy food, clean air, and lots of places to go fishing. So claim your birthright, and your children's. Claim it in living rooms, at church, in barbershops, and hair salons. This is how movements begin.

CAPITALISTS

You more than anyone know the tricks of capitalism. You know how to turn a little money into a wad. (Most of these tricks involve taking something from a commons.) But later, when you count your takings, do you think you merited every dollar? Or do you sometimes wonder, "Did I, or do I, get too much?"

Well, let me be blunt: you *do* get too much. But don't get your dander up; I'm not saying you're a scoundrel. I'm saying, rather, that capitalism as we know it over-rewards people who own private property. It's a *system* flaw, not a personal flaw. Its harm lies not so much in the luxuries it bestows on you as in the necessities it denies to others and the distortions it brews throughout society.

I don't expect you to surrender all your excess rewards at once. That would be asking more of you than I'm prepared to ask of myself. But I do ask you to consider doing two things: (1) Give back some of your excess takings now, and the rest when you die. And (2), if fellow citizens ask for a system upgrade that rewards noncapital owners more fairly, don't fight them. Let them have it. It will work. And it will be good for your kids and the planet.

COMMONS ENTREPRENEURS

You're going to change the world. You will build the new commons sector, one piece at a time. You'll be the unsung, or modestly sung, heroes and heroines of Capitalism 3.0.

A commons entrepreneur, like a private entrepreneur, is a visionary, a catalyst, a starter. You see a need that isn't being met, and a way to meet it. You bring people together, come up with a plan, and make it happen. Sometimes it works, sometimes it doesn't. The difference is, a commons entrepreneur doesn't get stock. You're motivated by a different force, *a desire to give back*. You aren't selfless; you enjoy success, recognition, and even money. But on balance, your desire to contribute to shared wealth outweighs your desire to accumulate private wealth. Accordingly, you choose the commons over the corporate sector.

A commons entrepreneur can work almost anywhere. Take a stroll around your neighborhood. What's missing? A community garden? A bike path? A wi-fi hot spot? A food-buying club? Make it happen! Whether your interests relate to a river, a form of culture, or the planet, get involved. Adopt a commons. Learn everything about it. Fall in love with it. See who's in charge. Then join or build an organization to revive it.

If you want a role model, consider Tim Berners-Lee, the inventor and promoter of the World Wide Web. Berners-Lee was a programmer at CERN, the European high-energy physics lab, when he had an idea to simplify the Internet through hypertext. Readers of an Internet page would simply click on a hypertext link and be transported automatically to another page, anywhere in the world. No more clunky protocols only geeks understand. Just one seamless information space, freely accessible to all.

Berners-Lee wrote the codes for Hypertext Transfer Protocol (HTTP) and Hypertext Markup Language (HTML). More importantly, he persuaded CERN to release them into the world with no patents, licenses, or other strings attached. This made it possible for anybody to adopt them without fear of lawsuits or ever having to pay a penny. Within a few years, the World Wide Web was ubiquitous. Berners-Lee then moved to MIT to lead an international consortium dedicated to preserving the Web as a nonproprietary space.

At numerous points along the way, Berners-Lee could have started or joined a business, and in all likelihood he would have reaped millions. At each point, he declined. "I wanted to see the Web proliferate, not sink my life's hours into worrying over a product release," he explained. Making a contribution to the commons was more important to him than taking out a bundle for himself.

As a commons entrepreneur, your work is more difficult than your corporate counterpart's. That's because you're treading in uncharted waters. The commons you seek to protect will probably lack property rights, and getting them can take years or decades. In fact, rounding up property rights will frequently be the first thing you do. That's in addition to rounding up money, which is tough enough.

Ultimately, you should strive to leave behind an institution that protects your beloved commons for generations to come. This is the measure of your success.

LAWYERS

You are the architects and defenders of property rights. You're well compensated by private property owners for your labors. Now is the time to lend more of your talents to the commons.

Your job is to design and defend *inclusive* forms of property that spread benefits to as many, rather than as few, as possible. To do this, you must play both defense and offense. On defense, be on high alert for "takings" from the commons—they happen all the time. I'm not talking about takings by government, but about takings by corporations, which occur far more frequently yet are much less noticed. Pollution is a taking, noise is a taking, capturing nature's scarcity rent is a taking. Your first job is to defend the commons against such enclosures.

Your second job—the offensive part—is to forge new property rights for the commons. These can be blends, like conservation easements. Be creative. Private and common property can often mesh together to the benefit of both. Making that happen is your gift.

ECONOMISTS

As a thought experiment, include common property trusts in your models. Imagine they're accountable to future generations and all living citizens equally. Imagine further, where appropriate, that they control valves that regulate aggregate use of scarce commons. Then play with quantities, prices, and income streams. If numerical precision isn't possible, use orders of magnitude. See what happens to GDP *and* the commons side of the ledger, to intra- and intergenerational equity, and to nature. Then report your findings to the world.

If you're not a modeler, work on institutional design. How should trusts be structured? What assets should they manage? What property rights should they own? Remember that property rights and operating systems aren't fixed forever. They're evolving social arrangements, and *you* can affect them.

RELIGIOUS LEADERS

We are of many faiths in America, yet we all agree on this: creation is sacred and humans are responsible for guarding it.

If we as a species are responsible for God's gifts, then we'd better get on with the job. Our current performance is disgraceful. We're fouling the air, pillaging the forests, mining the oceans, and killing species at an ungodly rate. A wrathful deity would strike us dead; a more compassionate one might merely melt the ice caps.

It's time to stop arguing over the history of creation and start focusing on its future. Its future, at this moment, looks grim. People of every faith, and of no faith, must join together to protect creation. This is at once an ecumenical and a holy task. If our species is to fulfill its special role as creation's guardian, we must immediately put our economic machine in order. Please help.

POLITICIANS

Everyone wants your attention. Channel 5 is on line 3 and a powerful lobbyist is at your door. It's hard for you to see the forest for the trees. What can I possibly tell you?

What I want to tell you is, there's a fork in the road. On one side lies capitalism as we know it; on the other, an upgrade. You must decide which branch to take. Your choice has vast ramifications. Very possibly, the fate of the planet is in your hands. Trillions of dollars are also at stake. I want you to be courageous. I want you to choose the upgrade.

But that isn't what one says to a politician. What one says is, we need to reduce our dependence on foreign oil, create jobs in America, and protect the environment. All those things cost money, and government doesn't have enough. But here's what government *can* do. First, delegate to an independent authority—something like the Fed—the power to cap U.S. carbon consumption. That way, when energy prices go up (which they inevitably will), you won't get blamed. Also, make sure the carbon authority pays dividends, like the Alaska Permanent Fund. Then, when checks are mailed to your constituents, you can take credit.

Second, talk about jobs and energy independence in your speeches. And push for an American Permanent Fund financed by sales of pollution permits. Within a few years, thousands of people in your district will be installing new energy systems *and* cashing dividend checks. You'll be a hero.

Finally, tell your donors not to worry. You're a low-tax, small-government, pay-as-we-go kind of person. You think the environment should be protected through market mechanisms. You favor an ownership society in which every American has a tax-deferred savings account and no child is left behind.

A New Economy for a New Era

The twenty-first century can't be a continuation of the twentieth. We're too close to too many tipping points for that.

But if it's not a continuation, what then? Then, it seems to me, we'll need a new economic operating system, because if we stick with the current one, huge bills will come due, tipping points will flip, and with some likelihood, things will spiral out of control.

The road to a new operating system isn't short or clearly lighted. We—meaning all of us together—will have to agree first on premises, and then on some basic design principles. We'll have to test theoretical models in the real world, then debug them as needed. Eventually, we'll have to scale up.

What I've sought to do in this book is to light this road. I've imagined a new operating system and called it Capitalism 3.0, though the name matters less than the substance. It involves balancing our selfish desires with our joint responsibilities, and embodying those responsibilities in our economic operating system.

What's particularly nice about Capitalism 3.0 is that we can install it one piece at a time. We needn't shut the machine down, or delete the old operating system, before installing the new one. Indeed, we're not even replacing most of the old operating system, which is fine as it is. Rather, we're attaching add-ons, or plug-ins, that allow for a gradual and safe transition. A formula for describing this is:

Corporations + Commons = Capitalism 3.0

Like the governor of James Watt's steam engine, these add-ons will curb our current engine's unchecked excesses. When illth of one sort gets too great, the new bits of code will turn the illth valve down, or give authority to trustworthy humans to do so. If money circulates too unequally, the new code will alter the circulation, not by *re*distributing income but by *pre*distributing property. It will make similar adjustments when there's too much corporate distortion of culture, communities, or democracy itself.

What's also nice about the new operating system is that, once installed, it can't be easily removed. That's because it relies on property rights rather than government programs that are subject to political ebb and flow. If you have any doubt about this, consider the staying power of Social Security and the Alaska Permanent Fund, both of which distribute periodic payments that have attained the status of property rights. Social Security is over seventy years old and has never been cut once; in 2005, it survived a privatization campaign led by President Bush. Similarly, the Alaska Permanent Fund, now more than twenty-five years old, repelled an attempt in 1999 to divert part of its income to the state treasury.

This third version of capitalism is a logical successor to the first two. In Capitalism 1.0 we had a shortage of goods, in Capitalism 2.0 a surplus. In Capitalism 3.0 we'll have plenty, but not too much. We'll have more things we truly need—healthier ecosystems, communities, culture—and fewer thneeds. We'll have a proper balance between our "me" and our "we" sides. We'll be more connected and less isolated, more secure and less stressed. Overall, I'd venture, we'll be happier.

We'll have some new traffic rules on this road. Rights now enjoyed exclusively by private capital will be matched, or even trumped, by rights held in trust for future generations. Similarly, the ability of private wealth owners to receive income and inheritances will be matched by the ability of everyone to receive them. And risks we now face individually, such as illness, will be tempered by shared risk pools that exclude no one.

The biggest change will be in the third algorithm I described in chapter 4: *the price of nature will no longer be zero.* Instead, the price of nature—or at least, of the scarcest and most endangered parts of nature—will gradually rise. This will compel corporations (and consumers) to internalize many of the costs they now externalize. This, in turn, will drive them to invest and consume in ways that, over time, do less harm to nature. Businesses will invest in clean and renewable energy technologies. Farmers will use fewer chemicals, and local food will outcompete food grown far away. Consumers will shift from driving alone in gas-guzzlers to more convivial forms of transport and less dashing about. Housing will move from sprawling suburbs to small towns and tall cities.

Not everything, however, will change. Winners in the marketplace will still enjoy privileges. Government won't overregulate our private lives or businesses. Nobody's private property will be expropriated. Markets will remain dynamic.

And, for businesspeople, here's the best part: Capitalism 3.0 will preserve the driving force of American capitalism, the profit-maximizing algorithm. It will do this not only by leaving the algorithm alone, but also by giving all Americans, via the American Permanent Fund, a financial stake in its success. All Americans will benefit *both* from nature's health and from the health of corporations.

Capitalism 2.0 had its moments. It defeated communism, leveled national boundaries to trade, and brought material abundance never seen before. But its triumph was accompanied by huge unpaid bills, debts that are now coming due.

Perhaps we ought to think of ourselves as a company in bankruptcy. We can't pay all of our bills, but we can pay some, especially if we stretch the payments out. In some cases, we can compensate debt holders with equity. In any event, we need to reorganize our economy so, in the future, we don't run up the same debts again. That's what Capitalism 3.0 would do.

But Capitalism 3.0 also has a higher purpose: to help both capitalism and the human species achieve their full potential. To do that, our economic machine must stop destroying the commons and start protecting it. At the same time, it must lift the bottom 95 percent of humans at a faster rate than it raises the top 5 percent. This requires more than compassionate rhetoric, or a few bandages around the edges. It requires an upgrade of our operating system.

I hope this book has shown how that can be done. It won't be easy, but we *can* do it. We have the know-how and the wealth. All we need now is the will.

Key Features of Corporate, State, and Commons Sectors

	CORPORATIONS	STATE	COMMONS
Key functions	Making things; seeking short-term profit	Defining, assigning, balancing rights	Sharing gifts and preserving them for future generations
Key institutions	Corporations; labor unions	Legislature Executive Judiciary	Ecosystem trusts, permanent funds, open access commons, intergenerational pacts, community commons
Key human actors	Directors	Politicians	Trustees
Accountable to	Share owners	Voters (donors)	Future generations, living citizens equally, nonhuman species, communities
Algorithms	Maximize profit; distribute earnings to existing shareholders	Win most votes (raise most money)	Preserve asset; live off income, not principal; follow the precautionary principle; the more beneficiaries the better
Time horizon	Next quarter	Next election	Next generation
Ownership regime	One dollar, one share	One person, one vote (one dollar, one vote)	One person, one share
Transferable ownership	Yes	Voting rights: No Property: Yes	Beneficial rights: No Usage rights: Yes
***From* each according to . . .**	Voluntary purchases	Taxes	Voluntary usage
***To* each according to . . .**	Share ownership	Political power	Equal ownership

Items in parentheses are *de facto*, not written in law.

Notes

Preface

x   **Biologist Garrett Hardin:** Garrett Hardin, "The Tragedy of the Commons," *Science,* 1968, 162, 1243–1248.
See www.sciencemag.org/sciext/sotp/commons.dtl.

xii   **envisioned an economy:** E. F. Schumacher, *Small Is Beautiful* (New York: HarperCollins, 1973).

Chapter 1: Time to Upgrade

4   **endangering human civilizations:** Jared Diamond, *Collapse: How Societies Choose to Fail or Succeed* (New York: Penguin Books, 2005); Ronald Wright, *A Short History of Progress* (New York: Carroll & Graf, 2004).

7   **"The relational herdsman . . .":** Hardin, "Tragedy of the Commons," p. 1244. Twenty-five years after this article was published, Hardin explained that what he *should* have said in 1968 was: "A 'managed commons' describes either socialism or the privatism of free enterprise. Either one may work; either one may fail: 'The devil is in the details.' But with an unmanaged commons, you can forget about the devil: As overuse of resources reduces carrying capacity, ruin is inevitable" (*Science,* May 1, 1998, p. 683). I don't find this "clarification" enlightening. If an "unmanaged commons" is inevitably self-destructive, and a "managed commons" is, by definition, either socialism or privatism, we are still left with only three alternatives: tragedy, statism, or privatism. In this book I describe a fourth alternative: trusteeship. See www.sciencemag.org/cgi/content/full/280/5364/682.

9   **feedback loops:** For some reason, scientists call virtuous feedback loops *negative* and vicious ones *positive.* I'll stick with the more intuitive adjectives.

9   **James Watt's design:** Here's how Watt's governor works. As the engine speeds up, a spindle spins faster and centrifugal force lifts two flyballs on hinged arms. This movement decreases the size of the air inlet valve, slowing the engine. Modern equivalents include thermostats on heaters, shutoff valves on toilets, and cruise control on cars.

10   **the Once-ler replies:** Theodor Seuss Geisel, *The Lorax* (New York: Random House, 1971).

Chapter 2: A Short History of Capitalism

16   **"For this labor . . .":** John Locke, *Second Treatise of Government* (Indianapolis: Hackett, 1980 [originally published 1690]), chapter 5, section 27.

17   **Privatization, the great transformation:** Karl Polanyi, *The Great Transformation: The Political and Economic Origins of Our Time* (Boston: Beacon Press, 1960 [originally published 1944]).

17   **"[Pay] to every person":** Thomas Paine, *Agrarian Justice* (http://geolib.pair.com/essays/paine.tom/agjst.html [originally published 1797]), sections i04, i05, 22 and 23.

19 **"It makes no sense . . .":** Bob Dole's statement on the spectrum giveaway can be found at www.anu.edu.au/mail-archives/link/link9601/0035.html. See also Ralph Kinney Bennett, "The Great Airwaves Giveaway," *Reader's Digest,* June 1996.

19 **"If you steal $10 . . .":** Walter Hickel, *Crisis in the Commons: The Alaska Solution* (Oakland, Calif.: ICS Press, 2002), p. 217.

20 **a handful of corporations:** Adam Smith, *The Wealth of Nations* (London: Penguin Books, 1982 [originally published 1776]).

21 **corporations were persons":** The Supreme Court decision that established corporate personhood was *Santa Clara County v. Southern Pacific Railroad,* 118 U.S. 394 (1886).

22 **Fortune 500 sales:** I computed the annual sales of Fortune 500 corporations from data available (for a fee) on *Fortune* magazine's website. See http://money.cnn.com/magazines/fortune/fortune500_archive/full/1955/index.htm.

23 **"So great has been the change . . .":** John Kenneth Galbraith, *The Affluent Society* (Boston: Houghton Mifflin, 1958), p. 2.

24 **scarce factor is trees:** See www.worldchanging.com/archives/004143.html.

25 **capitalism's stages:** I'm pleased to note that ecological economist Herman Daly has a two-stage schema similar to mine. Daly's focus is on the world in which the human economy resides. His dividing line is between an "empty world" and a "full world." In the former, nature is abundant; in the latter, it's scarce.

25 **consequences of ecosystem overuse:** Millennium Ecosystem Assessment, *Ecosystems and Human Well-Being: Synthesis Report* (Washington, D.C.: Island Press, 2005), p. 1.

26 **U.S. ecosystem damage figures:** Total CO_2 emissions from fossil fuel use and cement production since 1451 equal 290 billion tons (http://cdiac.ornl.gov/trends/emis/tre_glob.htm). U.S. historical emissions have been 84 billion tons since 1800 (http://cdiac.ornl.gov/ftp/trends/emissions/usa .dat). Thus, the proportion attributable to U.S. use is 29 percent.

28 **welfare keeps the poor poor:** Charles Murray, *Losing Ground: American Social Policy, 1950–1980* (New York: Basic Books, 1984).

28 **how corporations finance growth:** Marjorie Kelly, *The Divine Right of Capital* (San Francisco: Berrett-Koehler, 2001), p. 33.

29 **marketable wealth gain in U.S. between 1983 and 1998:** Edward N. Wolff, "The Rich Get Richer," *American Prospect,* Feb. 12, 2001. www.prospect.org/print/V12/3/wolff-e.html.

29 **General Social Survey:** Richard Layard, "Happiness: Has Social Science a Clue?" Lionel Robbins Memorial Lecture, Mar. 3–5, 2003, London School of Economics. http://cep.lse.ac.uk/events/lectures/layard/RL030303.pdf.

30 **marketing messages:** Michael Brower and Warren Leon, *The Consumer's Guide to Effective Environmental Choices: Practical Advice from the Union of Concerned Scientists* (New York: Three Rivers Press, 1999). www.ucsusa.org/assets/documents/ucs/CG-Chapter-1.pdf.

Chapter 3: The Limits of Government

33 *statism* and *privatism*: Hardin, "Tragedy of the Commons."

35 **regulatory capture:** Richard Posner, "Theories of Economic Regulation," *Bell Journal of Economics and Management Science,* Autumn 1974; George Stigler, "The Theory of Economic Regulation," *Bell Journal of Economics and Management Science,* Spring 1971; Gabriel Kolko, *The Triumph of Conservatism* (New York: Free Press, 1963); Mancur Olson, *The Logic of Collective Action* (Cambridge, Mass: Harvard University Press), 1965.

36 **U.S. governement officials:** Robert F. Kennedy Jr., *Crimes Against Nature: How George W. Bush and His Corporate Pals Are Plundering the Country and Hijacking Our Democracy* (New York: HarperCollins, 2004), p. 32.

36 **"influence industry":** Alex Knott, *Special Report: Industry of Influence Nets More Than $10 Billion* (Washington, D.C.: Center for Public Integrity, 2005). www.publicintegrity.org/lobby/report.aspx?aid=675.

36 **MBNA lobbying:** Courtney Mabeus, "Big Donors Go for Broke with Bankruptcy Bill," *Bankruptcy Reform News,* Mar. 4, 2005. www.bankruptcyfinder.com/article%20folder/bigdonors2005.html.

36 **lobbyists' behavior:** Philip Shenon, "Lobbying Campaign Led by Credit Card Companies and Banks Nears Bankruptcy Bill Goal," *New York Times,* Mar. 13, 2001.

37 **pharmaceutical lobbying:** Jim Drinkard, "Drugmakers Go Furthest to Sway Congress," *USA Today,* Apr. 26, 2005.

37 **broadcasting lobbying:** Kevin Phillips, *Wealth and Democracy: A Political History of the American Rich* (New York: Broadway Books, 2002), p. 326.

39 **using taxes to promote nature:** Arthur C. Pigou, *The Economics of Welfare* (London: Macmillan, 1920).

40 **Federal Reserve Board:** See www.federalreserve.gov/bios/default.htm.

44 **"has been hiding the ball . . .":** Sally Fairfax, *Lessons for the Forest Service from the State Trust Land Management Experience* (Washington, D.C.: Resources for the Future, 1999), Discussion Paper 99–16, pp. 22–23. www.rff.org/Documents/RFF-DP-99-16.pdf.

45 **Alaska couldn't discriminate:** *Zobel v. Williams,* 457 U.S. 55, 1982.

46 **Economist Vernon Smith:** Sean Butler, "Life, Liberty, and a Little Bit of Cash," *Dissent,* Summer 2005. www.dissentmagazine.org/article/?article=211.

Chapter 4: The Limits of Privatization

52 **". . . a license to obfuscate.":** Clive Cook, "The Good Company," *The Economist,* Jan. 20, 2005.

53 **Hurwitz:** Ned Daly, "Ravaging the Redwoods: Charles Hurwitz, Michael Milken, and the Costs of Greed," *Multinational Monitor,* Sept. 1994. www.multinationalmonitor.org/hyper/issues/1994/09/mm0994_07.html. See also David Harris, *The Last Stand: The War Between Wall Street and Main Street Over California's Ancient Redwoods* (San Francisco: Sierra Club Books, 1997).

54 **Working Assets:** *Report on Socially Responsible Investing Trends in the United States* (Washington, D.C.: Social Investment Forum, 2005). www.socialinvest.org/areas/research/trends/sri_trends_report_2005.pdf.

55 **Fortune 500 companies socially responsible?** Paul Hawken, "Is Your Money Where Your Heart Is? The Truth About SRI Mutual Funds," *Common Ground,* Oct. 2004, p. 14. www.responsibleinvesting.org/database/ dokuman/SRI _10-04_DragonflyMed.pdf.

55 **shareholder file resolutions:** *Report on Socially Responsible Investing Trends.*

58 **origins of free market environmentalism:** Ronald Coase, "The Problem of Social Cost," *Journal of Law and Economics,* Oct. 1960, pp. 1–44. www.sfu.ca/~allen/CoaseJLE1960.pdf.

59 **polluters trespassing on common property:** Kennedy, *Crimes Against Nature,* p. 190.

Chapter 5: Reinventing the Commons

66 **private wealth:** *Statistical Abstract of the United States, 2006* (Washington, D.C.: U.S. Census Bureau, 2006), Table 703. www.census.gov/prod/2005pubs/06statab/income.pdf.

70 **ecosystem services:** Robert Costanza and Paul Sutton, "Global Estimates of Market and Non-Market Values Derived from Nighttime Satellite Imagery, Land Cover, and Ecosystem Service Valuation," *Ecological Economics,* June 2002, pp. 509–527. www.uvm.edu/giee/research/publications/Sutton_and_Costanza.pdf.

71 **Internet income:** *Measuring the Internet Economy* (Austin: Cisco Systems and the University of Texas, Jan. 2001). www.momentumresearchgroup.com/ downloads/reports/internet-indicators-2001.pdf.

71 **Internet not-for-profit income:** *Arts and Economic Prosperity: The Economic Impact of Nonprofit Arts Organizations and Their Audiences* (Washington, D.C.: Americans for the Arts, 2002). http://pubs.artsusa.org./library/ARTS095/html.

74 **"enough and as good":** Locke, *Second Treatise.*

Chapter 6: Trusteeship of Creation

79 **"God gave the care of his earth . . .":** from *An Evangelical Call to Civic Responsibility,* 2004.

80 **"At an intersection . . .":** *California Drivers Handbook* (Sacramento: California Department of Motor Vehicles, 2006), p. 16. www.dmv.ca.gov/pubs/dl600.pdf.

80 **capital trumps everything:** Kelly, *Divine Right of Capital.*

81 **societieis choose top right holders:** To extend the driving analogy: in the twentieth century, thirty countries changed the side of the road they drive on (almost all switched from left to right.) Like choosing dominant property rights, choosing which side to drive on is a social choice, and society can change its mind.

82 **farmers vs. endangered fish:** Juliet Eilperin, "Water Rights Case Threatens Species Protection," *Washington Post,* Dec. 7, 2004, p. A18. www.washingtonpost.com/ac2/wp-dyn/A41450-2004Dec6?language=printer.

83 **Trebah Garden Trust:** For more information on Trebah Gardens, see www.trebahgarden.co.uk.

83 **Trusts:** Duties of trustees are described at www.trustland.org/about/responsibilities.cfm.

83 **Trustee duties:** Cardozo's statement on the fiduciary duty of trustees was made while sitting on the New York Court of Appeals in the case of *Meinhard v. Salmon,* 249 N.Y. 458 (1928).

84 **world-wide trusts:** For information on Britain's National Trust, see www.nationaltrust.org.uk. For information on the Nature Conservancy, see www.nature.org. For data about other land trusts in the United States, see the Land Trust Alliance's 2003 National Land Trust Census at www.lta.org/census/.

87 **carbon dioxide use:** Peter Barnes, *Who Owns the Sky? Our Common Assets and the Future of Capitalism* (Washington, D.C.: Island Press, 2001).

90 **farmer vs. cattle-raiser::** Coase, "The Problem of Social Cost," p. 2.

94 **American economist:** Henry George, *Progress and Poverty* (New York: Cosimo Classics, 2005 [originally published 1880]).

96 **common goods vs. public goods:** I must confess that, much as I like public goods, I don't like the idea of funding them with commons rent. I think commons rent should be distributed to owners, just as corporate income is, and that all personal income, regardless of source, should then be taxed at progressive rates to pay for public goods. Diverting commons rent to public goods is a hidden tax on the poor and an additional gift to the rich.

99 **Voters can "fire" elected officials":** See especially *Federalist Paper #10,* "The Union as a Safeguard Against Domestic Faction and Insurrection," *New York Packet,* Nov. 23, 1787. This paper discusses the danger of factions and how the Constitution is designed to mitigate it through checks and balances. www.foundingfathers.info/federalistpapers/fed10.htm.

Chapter 7: Universal Birthrights

103 **"The aim is not to guarantee . . .":** George Will, "Field of Dollars," *Washington Post,* Feb. 28, 1999, p. B7.

105 *redistribution vs. predistribution:* John Rawls, *A Theory of Justice* (Cambridge, Mass.: Harvard University Press, 1971).

106 **Less pollution = more revenue:** At this moment, the federal government and several states are giving corporate polluters free rights to use the atmosphere. It may seem shocking that politicians would create new property rights from a shared inheritance and give these valuable assets to a few corporations, yet that's what they're doing.

108 **"[T]he estates . . .":** For text of the Northwest Ordinance of 1787, see www.historicaldocuments.com /NorthwestOrdinance.htm. The quote is from section 2.

109 **interest earned by trust funds:** For information about Britain's "baby bonds," see "Saving from Birth: Baby Bonds Are a Great Radical Idea," *The Guardian,* Apr. 11, 2003. http://society.guardian.co.uk/publicfinances/comment/ 0,,934537,00.html. See also Stuart White (ed.), *The Citizen's Stake: Exploring the Future of Universal Asset Policies* (Bristol, U.K.: Policy Press, 2006).

112 **weathy's debt:** Bill Gates Sr.'s quote is taken from a forum at the Urban
Institute on Jan. 14, 2003, and can be found at
http://taxpolicycenter.org/publications/template.cfm?PubID=8248.

114 **per capital expenditures:** Stephen Heffler, Sheila Smith, Sean Keehan,
Christine Borger, M. Kent Clemens and Christopher Truffer, "U.S. Health
Spending Projections for 2004–2014," *Health Affairs,* Feb. 23, 2005.

114 **percent spent on administration:** Steffie Woolhandler, Terry Campbell, and
David Himmelstein, "Costs of Health Care Administration in the U.S. and
Canada," *New England Journal of Medicine,* Aug. 21, 2003.

114 **life expectancy:** *CIA World Factbook,* 2006,
www.cia.gov/cia/publications/factbook/.

116 **U.S. health insurance:** For information on obesity, diabetes, and depression
see www.newstarget .com. For data on health insurance coverage in the
United States, see *Income, Poverty, and Health Insurance Coverage in the United
States: 2003* (Washington, D.C.: U.S. Census Bureau, Aug. 2004), p. 14.
www.census.gov/prod /2004pubs/p60-226.pdf. For information about health
care costs in the United States, see Paul Krugman, "The Medical Money Pit,"
New York Times, Apr. 15, 2005, op ed page.

Chapter 8: Sharing Culture

118 **public domain:** On the Statute of Queen Anne, see
http://en.wikipedia.org/wiki/Statute_of_Anne. For more information on
the public domain see the website of the Center for the Study of the Public
Domain at Duke Law School, www.law.duke.edu/cspd/index.html.

119 **public domain:** Paul Starr, *The Creation of the Media* (New York: Basic
Books), p. 118.

122 **"Our mental environment . . .":** Kalle Lasn, *Culture Jam: The Uncooling
of America* (New York: William Morrow, 1999), p. 13.

122 **"feel constantly bombarded . . .":** Stuart Elliott, "New Survey on Ad
Effectiveness," *New York Times,* Apr. 14, 2004.
www.nytimes.com/2004/04/14/business/media/14adco.html?ex=1146110400
&en=89e6a892cb8b31c8&ei=5070. For more advertising data, see
www1.medialiteracy.com/stats_advertising.jsp#perceptions.

123 **TV advertising:** Gary Levin, "Ad Glut Turns Off Viewers," *USA Today,*
Oct. 12, 2005.
www.usatoday.com/printedition/life/20051012/d_cover12.art.htm.

125 **privatizing the airwaves:** For Lowell Paxson's quote, see
www.tvtechnology.com/features/Bigpicture/f-FB-DTV.shtml.

128 **"As we enjoy great advantages . . .":** For Benjamin Franklin's quote, see
http://en.wikipedia.org/wiki/Franklin_stove.

129 **drug costs to consumers:** Dean Baker, "The Reform of Intellectual Property,"
Post-Autistic Economics Review, July 2005.
www.paecon.net/PAEReview/issue32/Baker32.htm.

Chapter 9: Building the Commons Sector

136 **land trusts:** See www.dsni.org/ for more on the Dudley Street Neighborhood
Initiative.

137 **surface water rights:** See www.owt.org/ for more information on the Oregon Water Trust.

139 **Portland public spaces:** For more information about Portland's street intersections, see http://cityrepair.org/about.html.

139 **Brooklyn time bank:** For more information on ElderPlan in Brooklyn and "time dollars" generally, see www.timedollar.org/.

140 **atmosphere is common property:** See www.rggi.org/. Go to www.rggi.org/docs/mcc_auctions_letter.pdf for Marc Breslow's quote.

140 **state emission changes:** Information about the Vermont law, the Massachusetts bill, and Spitzer's statement can be found at www.massclimateaction.org/RGGI /RGGI.htm.

141 **The problem is** *hypoxia*: For information about the Mississippi Basin and hypoxia, see www.epa.gov/msbasin/.

142 *Buffalo Commons*: Frank and Deborah Popper, "The Great Plains: From Dust to Dust," *Planning*, Dec. 1987. www.planning.org/25anniversary/planning/1987dec.htm.

145 **market value of airwave licenses:** For an estimate of the value of public spectrum given free to broadcasters, download the New America Foundation's *Citizen's Guide to the Airwaves* at www.newamerica.net/index.cfm?sec= programs&pg=spectrum_direct&bg=blk&continue=yes&X_TRANTYPE= download.

149 *contract and converge*: For information on contract and converge, see the website of the London-based Global Commons Institute at www.gci.org.uk/main.html.

150 **a global atmosphere trust:** The 1919 Treaty of Versailles, drawn up at the close of World War I, carved up the Ottoman and Austro-Hungarian empires, set up the League of Nations, and imposed stiff reparations on Germany. Some believe it paved the way to World War II.

Chapter 10: What You Can Do

159 **"I wanted to see the Web proliferate . . .":** Tim Berners-Lee, *Weaving the Web* (San Francisco: HarperSanFrancisco, 1999), p. 84.

164 **Alaska Permanent Fund:** In 1999, Alaska's budget was in the red, and rather than raise taxes or cut expenditures, legislators tried to raid the Permanent Fund. After, however, voters in a referendum rejected their plan by 84 to 16 percent, the politicians gave up. "Voters Say Loud, Clear 'No,'" *Anchorage Daily News*, Sept. 15, 1999, p. A1.

Web Resource Guide

Tomales Bay Institute

The best overall website for ideas and commentaries on the commons is sponsored by the Tomales Bay Institute (www.onthecommons.org).

Public Knowledge

Public Knowledge advocates for balance between the rights of artists, writers, and other creators of culture on the one hand, and the public's right to the cultural commons on the other (www.publicknowledge.org).

Creative Commons

If you've written, filmed, photographed, or recorded something that you would like to publish, Creative Commons offers licenses that reserve some rights to you, the creator of the work, but share other rights with the public. The specific combination is up to you (http://creativecommons.org). Scientists might be interested in the companion site (http://sciencecommons.org), which tackles these issues for academics.

Land Trust Alliance and Pacific Forest Trust

The Land Trust Alliance can help you find a land trust operating in your area, and offers training to member trusts in how to be more effective at conserving land for future generations (www.lta.org). Readers looking to conserve working forests (those still subject to timber harvest) will find useful materials on stewardship forestry put out by Pacific Forest Trust (www.pacificforest.org).

American Community Gardening Association

Looking to find or start a community garden in your neighborhood? The American Community Gardening Association can help (http://communitygarden.org).

City Repair Project

The City Repair Project specializes in creating convivial public spaces within the urban environment. Its website includes inspiring examples and links to groups across the country that do similar work (www.cityrepair.org).

Center for Digital Democracy

The Center for Digital Democracy fights to maintain and expand the diversity of freely available resources on the Internet (www.democraticmedia.org).

Time Dollars

The commons of community can manifest itself through the exchange of time spent helping neighbors. Time Dollars has developed a system to keep track of those contributions (www.timedollar.org).

Public Spaces

The Project for Public Spaces has been helping cities and communities create vibrant public spaces for over 30 years. Its website (www.pps.org) has an amazing collection of images that reflect the many ways public spaces help people connect.

Global Atmospheric Commons

The London-based Global Commons Institute is the leading advocate of per capita sharing of the global atmospheric commons. Its website (www.gci.org.uk) explains the 'contract and converge' concept elegantly.

A Note of Caution

Beware of imitations! Several groups that associate themselves with the commons have little to do with the forms of managed, protected commons described in this book. A leading example is the blog "The Commons: Free Markets Protecting the Environment," which turns a blind eye to the excesses of unchecked corporations (www.commonsblog.org).

For a slightly different approach see EcoEquity (www.ecoequity.org).

Bibliography

The number of books that have been written about capitalism, the commons, and economic theory, is staggering. Below, I list books I have drawn upon in the text or that have significantly contributed to my thinking. Articles are referenced in the Notes section.

Ackerman, Bruce, and Anne Alstott. *The Stakeholder Society.* New Haven, Conn.: Yale University Press, 1999.

Agarwal, Anil, Sunita Narain, and Anju Sharma. *Green Politics: Global Environmental Negotiations.* New Delhi: Centre for Science and the Environment, 1999.

Alperowitz, Gar. *America Beyond Capitalism: Reclaiming Our Wealth, Our Liberty, and Our Democracy.* New York: Wiley, 2005.

Anderson, Terry, and Donald Leal. *Free Market Environmentalism.* San Francisco: Pacific Research Institute, 1991.

Ashworth, William. *The Economy of Nature: Rethinking the Connections Between Ecology and Economics.* Boston: Houghton Mifflin, 1995.

Athanasiou, Tom. *Divided Planet: The Ecology of Rich and Poor.* Boston: Little Brown, 1996.

Baden, John, and Douglass Noonan (eds.). *Managing the Commons.* Bloomington: Indiana University Press, 1998.

Bakan, Joel. The Corporation: *The Pathological Pursuit of Profit and Power.* New York: Free Press, 2004.

Baker, Dean, and Mark Weisbrot. *Social Security: The Phony Crisis.* Chicago: University of Chicago Press, 1999.

Barlow, Maude, and Tony Clarke. *Blue Gold: The Fight to Stop the Corporate Theft of the World's Water.* New York: New Press, 2003.

Barnes, Peter. *Who Owns the Sky? Our Common Assets and the Future of Capitalism.* Washington, D.C.: Island Press, 2001.

Berners-Lee, Tim. *Weaving the Web: The Original Design and Ultimate Destiny of the World Wide Web.* New York: HarperCollins, 2000.

Bollier, David. *Silent Theft: The Private Plunder of Our Common Wealth.* New York: Routledge, 2002.

Bollier, David. *Brand Name Bullies: The Quest to Own and Control Culture.* New York: Wiley, 2005.

Boyce, James (ed.). *Natural Assets: Democratizing Environmental Ownership.* Washington, D.C.: Island Press, 2003.

Brown, Peter. *Restoring the Public Trust: A Fresh Vision for Progressive Government in America.* Boston: Beacon Press, 1994.

Brown, Peter. *The Commonwealth of Life: A Treatise on Stewardship Economics.* Montreal: Black Rose Books, 2001.

Buck, Susan. *The Global Commons.* Washington, D.C.: Island Press, 1998.

Cavanagh, John, and Jerry Mander (eds.). *Alternatives to Economic Globalization: A Better World Is Possible.* San Francisco: Berrett-Koehler, 2002.

Coase, Ronald. *Essays on Economics and Economists.* Chicago: University of Chicago Press, 1994.

Collins, Chuck (ed.). *The Wealth Inequality Reader.* Cambridge, Mass.: Economic Affairs Bureau, 2004.

Collins, Chuck, and Felice Yeskel. *Economic Apartheid in America: A Primer on Economic Inequality and Security.* New York: New Press, 2000.

Daily, Gretchen (ed.). *Nature's Services: Societal Dependence on Natural Ecosystems.* Washington, D.C.: Island Press, 1997.

Daily, Gretchen, and Katherine Ellison. *The New Economy of Nature: The Quest to Make Conservation Profitable.* Washington, D.C.: Island Press, 2002.

Dales, J. H. Pollution, *Property and Prices.* Toronto: University of Toronto Press, 1968.

Daly, Herman (ed.). *Economics, Ecology, Ethics: Essays Toward a Steady-State Economy.* San Francisco: Freeman, 1980.

Daly, Herman. *Beyond Growth.* San Francisco: Freeman, 1997.

Daly, Herman, and John Cobb, Jr. *For the Common Good.* Boston: Beacon Press, 1989.

Daly, Herman, and Joshua Farley. *Ecological Economics: Principles and Applications.* Washington, D.C.: Island Press, 2003.

Darley, Julian. *High Noon for Natural Gas: The New Energy Crisis.* White River Junction, Vt.: Chelsea Green Press, 2005.

De Graaf, John (ed.). *Take Back Your Time.* San Francisco: Berrett-Koehler, 2003.

Diamond, Jared. *Collapse: How Societies Choose to Fail or Succeed.* New York: Penguin Books, 2005.

The Ecologist. *Whose Common Future? Reclaiming the Commons.* Gabriola Island, B.C.: New Society Publishers, 1993.

Fairfax, Sally, and Darla Guenzler. *Conservation Trusts.* Lawrence: University Press of Kansas, 2001.

Fairfax, Sally, and Jon Souder. *State Trust Lands: History, Management, and Sustainable Use.* Lawrence: University Press of Kansas, 1996.

Foster, John Bellamy. *The Vulnerable Planet: A Short Economic History of the Environment.* New York: Monthly Review Press, 1994.

Freyfogle, Eric. *The Land We Share.* Washington, D.C.: Island Press, 2003.

Galbraith, John Kenneth. *The Affluent Society.* Boston: Houghton Mifflin, 1958.

Gates, Bill Sr., and Chuck Collins. *Wealth and Our Commonwealth: Why America Should Tax Accumulated Fortunes.* Boston: Beacon Press, 2003.

Geisel, Theodor Seuss. *The Lorax.* New York: Random House, 1971.

Geisler, Charles, and Gail Daneker (eds.). *Property and Values: Alternatives to Public and Private Ownership.* Washington, D.C.: Island Press, 2000.

Gelbspan, Ross. *The Heat Is On: The Climate Crisis, the Cover-Up, the Prescription.* Reading, Mass.: Addison-Wesley, 1997.

George, Henry. *Progress and Poverty.* New York: Robert Schalkenbach Foundation, 1966. (Originally published 1880)

Gladwell, Malcolm. *The Tipping Point: How Little Things Can Make a Big Difference.* Boston: Little Brown, 2000.

Glennon, Robert. *Water Follies: Groundwater Pumping and the Fate of America's Fresh Waters.* Washington, D.C.: Island Press, 2003.

Glover, Linda, and Sylvia Earle (eds.). *Defying Ocean's End.* Washington, D.C.: Island Press, 2004.

Gore, Al. *Earth in the Balance.* Boston: Houghton Mifflin, 1992.

Greider, William. *The Soul of Capitalism: Opening Paths to a Moral Economy.* New York: Simon & Schuster, 2003.

Hammond, Jay. *Tales of Alaska's Bush Rat Governor.* Fairbanks: Epicenter Press, 1996.

Hardin, Garrett. *Nature and Man's Fate.* New York: Holt, Rinehart and Winston, 1959.

Harris, David. *The Last Stand: The War Between Wall Street and Main Street Over California's Ancient Redwoods.* San Francisco: Sierra Club Books, 1997.

Hartmann, Thom. *Unequal Protection: The Rise of Corporate Dominance and the Theft of Human Rights.* Emmaus, Penn.: Rodale Press, 2002.

Hawken, Paul. *The Ecology of Commerce.* New York: HarperCollins, 1993.

Hawken, Paul, Amory Lovins, and L. Hunter Lovins. *Natural Capitalism: Creating the Next Industrial Revolution.* Boston: Little Brown, 1999.

Heal, Geoffrey. *Nature and the Marketplace: Capturing the Value of the Ecosystem.* Washington, D.C.: Island Press, 2000.

Heilbroner, Robert. *The Worldly Philosophers.* New York: Touchstone Books, 1987.

Heilbroner, Robert. *21st Century Capitalism.* New York: W. W. Norton, 1993.

Heinberg, Richard. *The Party's Over: Oil, War and the Fate of Industrial Societies.* Gabriola Island, B.C.: New Society Publishers, 2005.

Hickel, Walter. *Crisis in the Commons: The Alaska Solution.* Oakland, Calif.: ICS Press, 2002.

Hill, Peter, and Roger Meiners (eds.). *Who Owns the Environment?* Lanham, Md.: Rowman & Littlefield, 1998.

Hyde, Lewis. *The Gift: Imagination and the Erotic Life of Property.* New York: Vintage Books, 1979.

Kelly, Marjorie. *The Divine Right of Capital.* San Francisco: Berrett-Koehler, 2001.

Kennedy, Robert F. Jr. *Crimes Against Nature: How George W. Bush and His Corporate Pals Are Plundering the Country and Hijacking Our Democracy.* New York: HarperCollins, 2004.

Keynes, John Maynard. *Essays in Persuasion.* New York: W. W. Norton, 1963. (Originally published 1930)

Keynes, John Maynard. *The General Theory of Employment, Interest and Money.* New York: Harcourt Brace, 1989. (Originally published in 1936)

Korten, David. *When Corporations Rule the World.* San Francisco: Berrett-Koehler, 1995.

Korten, David. *The Post-Corporate World: Life After Capitalism.* San Francisco: Berrett-Koehler, 2002.

Kunstler, James Howard. *The Long Emergency.* New York: Atlantic Monthly Press, 2005.

Kuttner, Robert. *Everything for Sale: The Virtues and Limits of Markets.* New York: Knopf, 1997.

Lasn, Kalle. *Culture Jam: The Uncooling of America.* New York: William Morrow, 1999.

Layard, Richard. *Happiness: Lessons from a New Science.* New York: Penguin Books, 2005.

Leopold, Aldo. *A Sand County Almanac.* New York: Oxford University Press, 1949.

Lessig, Lawrence. *The Future of Ideas: The Fate of the Commons in a Connected World.* New York: Vintage Books, 2001.

Lessig, Lawrence. *Free Culture: How Big Media Uses Technology and the Law to Lock Down Culture and Control Creativity.* New York: Penguin Books, 2004.

Linden, Eugene. *The Future in Plain Sight: Nine Clues to the Coming Instability.* New York: Simon & Schuster, 1998.

Locke, John. *Second Treatise of Government.* Indianapolis: Hackett, 1980. (Originally published 1690)

Lovelock, James. *Gaia: A New Look at Life on Earth.* Oxford, England: Oxford University Press, 1979.

Lovelock, James. *Healing Gaia: Practical Medicine for the Planet.* New York: Crown, 1991.

Marsh, George Perkins. *Man and Nature.* New York: Scribner's, 1882.

Mayer, Carl, and George Riley. *Public Domain, Private Domain: A History of Public Mineral Policy in America.* San Francisco: Sierra Club Books, 1985.

McKibben, Bill. *The End of Nature.* New York: Random House, 1989.

McNeil, J. R. *Something New Under the Sun.* New York: W. W. Norton, 2000.

Meadows, Donella, et al. *The Limits to Growth.* New York: Universe Books, 1972.

Meadows, Donella, Dennis Meadows, and Jørgen Randers. *Beyond the Limits.* White River Junction, Vt.: Chelsea Green Press, 1992.

Millennium Ecosystem Assessment. *Ecosystems and Human Well-Being: Synthesis Report.* Washington, D.C.: Island Press, 2005.

Monbiot, George. *Manifesto for a New World Order.* New York: New Press, 2004.

Murray, Charles. *Losing Ground: American Social Policy, 1950–1980.* New York: Basic Books, 1984.

Nordhaus, William D. *Managing the Global Commons: The Economics of Change.* Cambridge, Mass.: MIT Press, 1994.

Olson, Mancur. *The Logic of Collective Action.* Cambridge, Mass.: Harvard University Press, 1965.

Ostrom, Elinor. *Governing the Commons.* New York: Cambridge University Press, 1990.

Parker, Richard. *John Kenneth Galbraith: His Life, His Politics, His Economics.* New York: Farrar, Straus and Giroux, 2005.

Phillips, Kevin. *Wealth and Democracy: A Political History of the American Rich.* New York: Broadway Books, 2002.

Pigou, Arthur C. *The Economics of Welfare.* London: Macmillan, 1920.

Polanyi, Karl. *The Great Transformation: The Political and Economic Origins of Our Time.* Boston: Beacon Press, 1960. (Originally published 1944)

Ponting, Clive. *A Green History of the World: The Environment and the Collapse of Great Civilizations.* New York: St. Martin's Press, 1992.

Porritt, Jonathon. *Capitalism As If the World Matters.* London: Earthscan/James & James, 2005.

Rawls, John. *A Theory of Justice.* Cambridge, Mass.: Harvard University Press, 1971.

Roodman, David Malin. *The Natural Wealth of Nations.* New York: W. W. Norton, 1998.

Rothschild, Michael. *Bionomics: The Inevitability of Capitalism.* New York: Holt, Rinehart and Winston, 1990.

Ruskin, John. *Unto This Last.* New York: Penguin Books, 1986. (Originally published 1860)

Sachs, Wolfgang. *Planet Dialectics: Explorations in Environment and Development.* London: Zed Books, 2000.

Scherf, Judith (ed.). *The Piracy of America: Profiteering in the Public Domain.* Atlanta: Clarity Press, 1999.

Schor, Juliet. *The Overworked American.* New York: Basic Books, 1993.

Schor, Juliet. *The Overspent American: Why We Want What We Don't Need.* New York: Basic Books, 1998.

Schumacher, E. F. *Small Is Beautiful: Economics as if People Mattered.* New York: HarperCollins, 1973.

Schweickart, David. *After Capitalism.* Lanham, Md.: Rowman & Littlefield, 2002.

Shanks, Bernard. *This Land Is Your Land.* San Francisco: Sierra Club Books, 1984.

Sherraden, Michael. *Assets and the Poor: A New American Welfare Policy.* Armonk, N.Y.: M. E. Sharpe, 1991.

Shiva, Vandana. *Biopiracy: The Plunder of Nature and Knowledge.* Cambridge, Mass.: South End Press, 1997.

Shiva, Vandana. *Water Wars: Privatization, Pollution, and Profit.* Cambridge, Mass.: South End Press, 2002.

Shiva, Vandana. *Earth Democracy: Justice, Sustainability, and Peace.* Cambridge, Mass.: South End Press, 2005.

Shulman, Seth. *Owning the Future.* Boston: Houghton Mifflin, 1999.

Simms, Andrew. *Ecological Debt: The Health of the Planet and the Wealth of Nations.* London: Pluto Press, 2005.

Smith, Adam. *The Wealth of Nations.* London: Penguin Books, 1982. (Originally published 1776)

Smith, Adam. *The Theory of Moral Sentiments.* Amherst, N.Y.: Prometheus Books, 2000. (Originally published 1759)

Steinberg, Theodore. *Slide Mountain: The Folly of Owning Nature.* Berkeley: University of California Press, 1995.

Stone, Christopher. *Should Trees Have Standing? Toward Legal Rights for Natural Objects.* Los Altos, Calif.: William Kaufman, 1974.

Stone, Christopher. *Earth and Other Ethics.* New York: HarperCollins, 1987.

Stone, Christopher. *The Gnat Is Older Than Man: Global Environment and Human Agenda.* Princeton: Princeton University Press, 1993.

Suzuki, David. *The Sacred Balance: Rediscovering Our Place in Nature.* Amherst, N.Y.: Prometheus Books, 1998.

Swann, Robert. "Land: Challenge in Opportunity." In William Vitek and Wes Jackson (eds.), *Rooted in the Land.* New Haven: Yale University Press, 1996.

Tudge, Colin. *The Time Before History: 5 Million Years of Human Impact.* New York: Simon & Schuster, 1997.

Washburn, Jennifer. *University, Inc.: The Corporate Corruption of Higher Education.* New York: Basic Books, 2005.

Weber, Max. *The Protestant Ethic and the Spirit of Capitalism.* New York: Scribner's, 1958. (Originally published 1904)

White, Stuart (ed.). *The Citizen's Stake: Exploring the Future of Universal Asset Policies.* Bristol, U.K.: Policy Press, 2006.

Wilson, E. O. *The Diversity of Life.* New York: W. W. Norton, 1993.

Wright, Ronald. *A Short History of Progress.* New York: Carroll & Graf, 2004.

Index

About the Author

Peter Barnes is an entrepreneur and writer who has founded and led several successful companies. At present he is a senior fellow at the Tomales Bay Institute in Point Reyes Station, California.

Barnes grew up in New York City and earned a B.A. in history from Harvard and an M.A. in government from Georgetown. He began his career as a reporter on *The Lowell Sun* (Massachusetts), and was subsequently a Washington correspondent for *Newsweek* and the West Coast correspondent for *The New Republic*.

In 1976 he cofounded a worker-owned solar energy company in San Francisco, and in 1983 he cofounded Working Assets Money Fund. He subsequently served as president of Working Assets Long Distance. In 1995 has was named Socially Responsible Entrepreneur of the Year for Northern California.

He has served on numerous boards of directors, including the National Cooperative Bank, the California State Assistance Fund for Energy, the California Solar Industry Association, Businesses for Social Responsibility, the Rainbow Workers Cooperative, Techmar, Redefining Progress, the Family Violence Prevention Fund, Public Media Center, TV-Turnoff Network, the Noise Pollution Clearing-house, Greenpeace International, the California Tax Reform Association, and the Center for Economic and Policy Research.

His previous books include *Pawns: The Plight of the Citizen-Soldier* (Knopf, 1972), *The People's Land* (Rodale, 1975), and *Who Owns the Sky? Our Common Assets and the Future of Capitalism* (Island Press, 2001). His articles have appeared in *The Economist,* the *New York Times,* the *Washington Post,* the *San Francisco Chronicle,* the *Christian Science Monitor, The American Prospect,* the *Utne Reader,* and elsewhere.

In 1997 he founded the Mesa Refuge, a writers' retreat in northern California. He has two sons, Zachary and Eli; a partner, Cornelia Durrant; and a dog, Smokey.

A Note on the Creative Commons Electronic License for This Book

A downloadable version of this book containing all text and permissable graphics is available at no charge at
http://www.onthecommons.org.

The electronic version of the work is licensed under the Creative Commons Attribution-NonCommercial-NoDerivs 2.5 License (some restrictions apply). To view a copy of this license, visit http://creativecommons.org/licenses/by-nc-nd/2.5/ or send a letter to Creative Commons, 543 Howard Street, 5th Floor, San Francisco, California, 94105, USA.

About Berrett-Koehler Publishers

Berrett-Koehler is an independent publisher dedicated to an ambitious mission: Creating a World that Works for All.

We believe that to truly create a better world, action is needed at all levels—individual, organizational, and societal. At the individual level, our publications help people align their lives with their values and with their aspirations for a better world. At the organizational level, our publications promote progressive leadership and management practices, socially responsible approaches to business, and humane and effective organizations. At the societal level, our publications advance social and economic justice, shared prosperity, sustainability, and new solutions to national and global issues.

A major theme of our publications is "Opening Up New Space." They challenge conventional thinking, introduce new ideas, and foster positive change. Their common quest is changing the underlying beliefs, mindsets, institutions, and structures that keep generating the same cycles of problems, no matter who our leaders are or what improvement programs we adopt.

We strive to practice what we preach—to operate our publishing company in line with the ideas in our books. At the core of our approach is *stewardship*, which we define as a deep sense of responsibility to administer the company for the benefit of all of our "stakeholder" groups: authors, customers, employees, investors, service providers, and the communities and environment around us.

We are grateful to the thousands of readers, authors, and other friends of the company who consider themselves to be part of the "BK Community." We hope that you, too, will join us in our mission.

A BK Currents Book

This book is part of our BK Currents series. BK Currents books advance social and economic justice by exploring the critical intersections between business and society. Offering a unique combination of thoughtful analysis and progressive alternatives, BK Currents books promote positive change at the national and global levels. To find out more, visit www.bkcurrents.com.

Be Connected

Visit Our Website

Go to www.bkconnection.com to read exclusive previews and excerpts of new books, find detailed information on all Berrett-Koehler titles and authors, browse subject-area libraries of books, and get special discounts.

Subscribe to Our Free E-Newsletter

Be the first to hear about new publications, special discount offers, exclusive articles, news about bestsellers, and more! Get on the list for our free e-newsletter by going to www.bkconnection.com.

Participate in the Discussion

To see what others are saying about our books and post your own thoughts, check out our blogs at www.bkblogs.com.

Get Quantity Discounts

Berrett-Koehler books are available at quantity discounts for orders of ten or more copies. Please call us toll-free at (800) 929-2929 or email us at bkp.orders@ aidcvt.com.

Host a Reading Group

For tips on how to form and carry on a book reading group in your workplace or community, see our website at www.bkconnection.com.

Join the BK Community

Thousands of readers of our books have become part of the "BK Community" by participating in events featuring our authors, reviewing draft manuscripts of forthcoming books, spreading the word about their favorite books, and supporting our publishing program in other ways. If you would like to join the BK Community, please contact us at bkcommunity @bkpub.com.

9 - Feedback loops
23 - Capitalism 1.0
73 - propertization not privatization
83 - Trusts